'That'll be the Day!'

1950s Newcastle

Memories from people who were there

Edited by Anna Flowers and Vanessa Histon

Tyne Bridge Publishing

Angela Evans

Tyne Bridge Publishing and Newcastle Libraries sincerely thank all our contributors, who gave so generously of their time, memories, photographs, and memorabilia. This book is by you, and for you. We were not able to include everything that was sent to us, and we apologise to those whose memories we could not fit in. We hope that the following pages give an authentic flavour of some of the things that mattered to the people of Newcastle in the 1950s. If it isn't here, then you didn't tell us about it!

Special thanks to ncjMedia Ltd, Procter & Gamble, Tyne & Wear Archives & Museums for permission to reproduce their evocative photographs. Our grateful thanks to retired librarian Douglas Bond for writing the introduction. Heartfelt thanks to everyone who helped with sourcing illustrations.

Photographs from 1950s student Martin Nellist were an unexpected and very welcome bonus. The trade tokens were loaned by Brian Fagleman.

Unless otherwise indicated illustrations are from the collections of, and are copyright of, Newcastle Libraries.

Front cover: Elspeth Rutter and art college friends on the Quayside, 1959. 'My friend Suzanne was a big hit with her net and hooped slip under her full skirt.' *(Elspeth Rutter/ncjMedia Ltd)*

Back cover central image: Newcastle Official Guide, 1956.

©Tyne Bridge Publishing, 2012

Published by
City of Newcastle upon Tyne
Newcastle Libraries & Information Service
Tyne Bridge Publishing, 2012

www.tynebridgepublishing.co.uk
www.newcastle.gov.uk/libraries

ISBN: 978-1-85795-210-0

Printed by blp (Northern) Ltd.

A milk token, used by many dairies. You'd put them under the return bottles at night, or in a container that snapped round the bottle neck.

The Close, left, and the Quayside, below, were photographed by student Martin Nellist in 1957.

This yellow plastic token, value 2d was used on Newcastle Corporation Tramways.

Previous page: typical 1950s curtain material from a Fenham household.

Shirt worn by Jackie Milburn in the 1951-52 season. 'Wor Jackie' was Newcastle's best loved number 9, scoring 239 goals in 494 appearances for the club. Milburn was part of the FA Cup winning teams of 1951, 1952 and 1955, and was capped for England 13 times.

The official football programme for Arsenal v Newcastle United FA Cup Final at Wembley on 3 May 1952. Newcastle clinched their second FA Cup in successive years, beating Arsenal 1-0.

A match ticket for the FA Cup Final at the Empire Stadium, Wembley, on 7 May 1955. Newcastle stormed to a 3-1 victory against Manchester City.

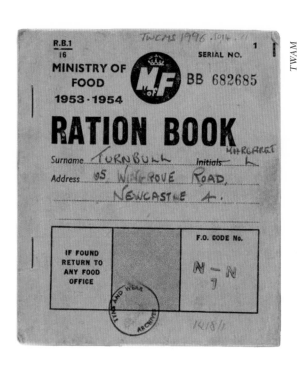

Ration books were introduced during World War 2 to control access to some foods because of shortages. Meats, eggs, fats, cheese, bacon and sugar are listed in the book. This ration book, owned by M.L. Turnbull of Newcastle, shows that they were still in use almost 10 years after the end of the war.

Top right, this 1953 photo from the Thomas Hedley staff magazine 'Moonbeams' pointed out that a Daz box could be recycled as a useful groceries container.

This portable television was made by E. K. Cole in 1954. Compared with other television sets of the time this one is small and light.

In October 1954, the year that rationing finally ended, Queen Elizabeth visited the North East, cheering everyone up despite the rain. The previous year thousands of Tynesiders had watched the Coronation on television, some on sets especially bought for the occasion, and many in neighbours' houses.

SMILING HAPPILY, the Queen walks with the Lord Mayor of Newcastle (Ald. R. Mould-Graham) at the Mansion House, where she and the Duke of Edinburgh had luncheon during today's tour.

Martin Nellist

Brian Sefton

These colour shots of the 1957 Rag Parade were taken on a 35mm Zeiss Ikon Contina 1a. This was poor relation of the famous Contax. It had a fixed 45mm lens which meant that the field of view was slightly wide angle. Photographer Martin Nellist, was a member of the King's College Camera Club: 'we had a darkroom on the second or third floor of a house in Leazes Terrace. The darkroom had some reasonable equipment but the rest of the building was derelict and coming and going could be rather eerie.'

The parade is passing the Students' Union on College Road.

Brian Sefton kept his 1958 Rag matchbook (for all those cigarettes).

Martin Nellist

Leila Eagleman

You might almost think this is a photo from the 2010s, but it isn't. Colour photographs of the city were quite rare in the 1950s. This one captures the top end of Northumberland Street in October 1957 as the Rag Parade got underway, with music from the lads with guitars.

The shops on the left are Edythe M. Pegg dressmaker, Pettie's hairdressers, Newcastle Breweries, Charles Sutherland gents outfitters, and Finlay's tobacconists. In the distance is the Crow's Nest pub. The sign on the lamp post by Finlay's affirms that this is indeed the A1.

The Arts Ball, right, was a regular university event.

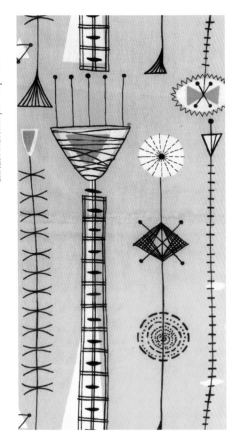

The shirt dress was a 1950s classic, cut fairly straight with a belt at the waist, or with a circle skirt. New materials like rayon, nylon, crimplene and orlon, were easy to look after, washable, and were soon affordable. White and pastel colours became popular. Crimplene also tailored well and the new styles kept a smart appearance after washing.

'Kite Strings', a fabric created for Heals by David Parsons in 1955 made a colourful pair of curtains for a Newcastle home. It was available in at least three colourways.

Tide, Daz, and Fairy Snow, all researched at Thomas Hedley's in Newcastle, as well as the advent of the washing machine, made wash day easier, and clothes easier to keep clean.

A popular fashion coat of the 1950s was the swing coat, good for covering full skirts, and often with a cowl neck or large collar. This style was also often made as a loose full tent line duster coat. Student Martin Nellist snapped this fashionable young crowd watching the 1957 Rag Parade. The wide angle shot makes the majorettes in the foreground seem giant!

The Beatnik look was an alternative, and fashion student Elspeth Rutter, below with her sister Kirsteen on the Quayside, was wearing a duffle coat and close-fitting jeans bought from Harker's Army and Navy Stores on Percy Street. Kirsteen's Sloppy Joe jumper completes the cool student look.

CITY HALL,
Northumberland Road, Newcastle upon Tyne, 1.

MONDAY, DECEMBER 1st, 1958
at 7-30 p.m.

DUNCAN MACKINNON
presents

Mr. ACKER BILK

PLATFORM 2/6   SEAT 21

Booking Agents: A. E. Cook, Limited, 5-6
Newcastle upon Tyne, 1. (Tel. 2-290
This Portion to be Retained.

Phillips Printers, Ltd., Trafalgar St., Newcastle-on-Tyne, 1.

CITY HALL
Northumberland Road, Newcastle upon Tyne, 1

THURSDAY, 6th MARCH, 1958
at 6-20 p.m.

ARTHUR HOWES presents

BUDDY HOLLY
AND THE CRICKETS

Area 8/6   Nº   28

Booking Agents: Waddington & Sons Ltd., Metrovick House,
Northumberland Road, Newcastle upon Tyne, 1
This portion to be retained

CITY HALL
Northumberland Road, Newcastle upon Tyne, 1.

SAT. MARCH 30TH, 1957, AT 7-30 P.M.

Arthur Howes presents

SKIFFLE and JAZZ CONCERT
ALL STAR

Area 5/-   Nº   27   F
Tax Included

Booking Agents:
Waddingtons, 24, Northumberland Rd., Newcastle-on-Tyne, 1

CITY HALL,
Northumberland Road, Newcastle upon Tyne, 1.

FRIDAY, MAY 30th, 1958
at 7.30 p.m.

ARTHUR HOWES
presents

Chris Barber's Jazz B
OTTILIE PATTERSON
SONNY TERRY   BROWNIE M   GO
SEAT

AREA 5/-

Booking Agents: Waddington & Sons,
House, Northumberland Road, Newcastle upon

Phillips Printers, Ltd., Trafalgar Street, Newcastle-on-Tyne

CITY HALL
Northumberland Road, Newcastle upon Tyne, 1.

WED. APRIL 10TH, 1957, AT 6-20 P.M.

Harold Fielding presents

COUNT BASIE
AND HIS ORCHESTRA

Balcony 10/6   Nº   18
Tax Included

Booking Agents:
Waddingtons, 24, Northumberland Rd., Newcastle

CITY HALL
Northumberland Road, Newcastle upon Tyne, 1

Wednesday, 30th September, 1959
at 8.40 p.m.

ARTHUR HOWES *presents*
(By arrangement with Harold Davison)

"NEWPORT JAZZ FESTIVAL"
(featuring
THE DAVE BRUBECK QUARTET   DIZZY GILLESPIE QUINTET
BUCK CLAYTON ALL STARS

PLATFORM 5/-   SEAT

Booking Agents: A. E. Cook Ltd, Record
Saville Place, Newcastle upon Tyne
This Portion t
2901)

Phillips Printers, Ltd., Trafalgar Street, Newcastle-on-Tyne

CITY HALL
NORTHUMBERLAND ROAD, NEWCASTLE UPON TYNE

Saturday, 18th October, 1958, at 7.30 p.m.

Arthur Howes presents

MUDDY WATERS
with CHRIS BARBER'S JAZZ BAND

Area 5/-   Nº   25   KK

Booking Agents: Laurence Hill (Ncle.) Ltd.,
1, Pink Lane, Newcastle upon Tyne, 1
This portion to be retained

CITY HALL,
Northumberland Road, Newcastle upon Tyne, 1

Wednesday, 13th May, 1959, at 8.40 p.m.

ARTHUR HOWES *presents*

NORMAN GRANZ'
"JAZZ AT THE PHILHARMONIC"
Starring ELLA FITZGERALD

PLATFORM 5/-

Booking Agents: A. E. Cook, Limited, 5-6, Saville Place,
Newcastle upon Tyne, 1. (Tel. 2-2901).
This Portion to be retained.

Phillips Printers, Ltd., Trafalgar Street, Newcastle-on-Tyne

An astonishing variety of performers could be seen at Newcastle City Hall in the 1950s. In 1957, for example, at least 69 shows were put on from Pat Boone to the Hallé, Count Basie and Chrismas carols.

During the winter months Northumberland Baths' swimming pool was boarded over and Scottish and 'Old Tyme' dancing was held.

HAROLD DAVISON & NORMAN GRANZ present

KID ORY
AND HIS CREOLE JAZZ BAND

SOUVENIR PROGRAMME · PRICE TWO SHILLINGS

JAZZSHOWS present

Sister ROSETTA THARPE

America's Greatest
GOSPEL SINGING and
GUITAR PLAYING STAR

SOUVENIR PROGRAMME
ONE SHILLING

CITY HALL,
Northumberland Road, Newcastle upon Tyne, 1.
FRIDAY, 8th MARCH, 1957,
at 7.30 p.m.
WHITLEY BAY S.C.D.S.
Presents
JIMMY SHAND
AND HIS BAND

AREA 5/-   SEAT M 14
(Tax Inclusive)

Booking Agents: Waddington & Sons, Ltd., Metrovick
House, Northumberland Road, Newcastle upon Tyne, 1.
This Portion to be Retained

CITY HALL
Northumberland Road, Newcastle upon Tyne, 1

SUNDAY, 9th MARCH, 1958
at 7-30 p.m.
VICTOR HOCHHAUSER presents
MARIO LANZA

Area 21/-   №   22 J

Booking Agents: Waddington & Sons Ltd., Metrovick House
Northumberland Road, Newcastle upon Tyne, 1
This portion to be retained

THE **PHILADELPHIA ORCHESTRA**

Conductor
EUGENE ORMANDY
"The finest orchestra the
world has ever known"
—Rachmaninoff

CITY HALL - NEWCASTLE
WEDNESDAY & THURSDAY, JUNE 1ST & 2ND, AT 7 P.M.
ONLY CONCERTS IN NEWCASTLE AND DISTRICT
OF THE FIRST AMERICAN SYMPHONY ORCHESTRA
TO VISIT EUROPE FOR TWENTY YEARS

BOOKING OPENS FRIDAY, MAY 13th
3/6 5/- 7/6 10/6 12/6 15/- 21/-
WADDINGTONS, NORTHUMBERLAND ROAD, NEWCASTLE
Telephone: 24279.

A two shilling trade token from A.E. Cook Ltd of Saville Place.

Above, a hand-coloured black and white postcard from the early 1950s shows Barras Bridge and the A1 just post-war.

By 1959 all the changes that would herald the 1960s and Newcastle's revolution in roads, housing, entertainment and education were in place.

Right, this radiogram was bought in 1957.

TWAM

Crowds gather on St Nicholas Square opposite Newcastle Town Hall on 8 February 1952 for the proclamation to the city of the accession of Queen Elizabeth II.

Northumberland Street, probably mid-1950s, so crowded that pedestrians are walking on the busy main road. The shop on the far left was Jay's Furnishing Stores, and the sunburst style clock (or mirror) in the window was a popular item from the early 1950s. A Bainbridge's van has just turned into Prudhoe Street beyond the Northumberland Arms.

Contents

A colour section is inserted between pages 144 and 145

Que Sera Sera

Doris Day, 1956

The 1950s in the wider world ...

The 1950s was a decade that witnessed great changes throughout the world. Still suffering from post-war austerity, there was great hope and optimism for the future, but also worry about continuing unrest in Europe, Africa, the Middle East and the Far East. Only five years after the second world war came to an end, war broke out again in the Far East when North Korea invaded South Korea, and the United States became involved when it gave backing to South Korea. This conflict dragged on until 1953 when an armistice was signed. Also in 1950, President Truman ordered the construction of a hydrogen bomb. In 1951, South Africans were forced to carry identity cards identifying their racial background, which led to great unrest on the African continent. The first atomic-powered submarine was launched in 1954. The Warsaw Pact was signed in 1955, leading to British Prime Minister Winston Churchill's famous 'an iron curtain has descended across Europe' speech. In the United States, Rosa Parks refused to give up her seat to a white woman on a bus, sparking the beginning of the American Civil Rights movement.

Two major events caused concern in 1956. When the people of Hungary rose up against their Russian masters, the revolution was crushed cruelly and brutally by Russian forces, and in the Middle East the Suez crisis caused problems around the world. Fidel Castro became President of Cuba in 1958, straining relations with the United States, and in the closing year of the decade, the United States agreed to supply South Vietnamese troops in that country's war with North Vietnam.

There were more hopeful signs in the Fifties as well. In Britain, the Clean Air Act was introduced as a result of the dreadful London smog of 1952, which had killed 4,000 people with a further 8,000 dying at a later date from the after-effects. In 1953, along with the Queen's Coronation, Mount Everest was finally conquered by Sir Edmund Hillary and Sherpa Tensing. The following year, Dr Roger Bannister broke the four-minute mile. In 1955, Disneyland opened in Anaheim, California. 1956 saw the fairytale wedding of the actress Grace Kelly and Prince Rainier III of Monaco. The following extraordinary event from 1956 was kept secret under the 30 year rule. France was suffering great economic hardship, and

Newcastle Journal
North Mail

No. 32,292   THURSDAY, JANUARY 19, 1950   A KEMSLEY NEWSPAPER   ONE PENNY

6 A.M. EDITION

POWER CUTS FOR FIVE YEARS

Homes, industry warned

Austria: 3-Power Note to Moscow

BRITISH, French and American representatives delivered a joint Note to M. Andrei Gromyko, Soviet Deputy Foreign Minister, about the Austrian Treaty negotiations.

The Note was delivered to him early in the morning, and was later sent to the Soviet Government.

TYSHINSKY ILL

NO PROGRESS

Offered Saar guarantee

FIRST PROFIT £4,000,000

BY AN INDUSTRIAL CORRESPONDENT

"LOAD SHEDDING," which means power cuts for industrial and domestic consumers, may continue until 1955 according to the British Electricity Authority.

It is stated in a report issued by the Authority to-day, that higher charges may be necessary unless more electricity can be sold.

This was the quandary with which the seven members of the British Electricity Authority confronted themselves to be faced at a London Press conference last night when the first annual report, which will be debated early in the life of the new Parliament, was presented.

Although electricity was nationalised on April 1, 1948, shows a profit of £4,301,484 on its first 12 months and a further profit is expected on the current year (ending March 31), increased costs of plant replacement may bring about higher charges.

FREE USE OF HOSTEL AS HOMES

Now in trouble

CONVERSIONS

Cost 'unknown'

LINO DOWN, CARPETS UP

Time lapse

Rare blood rushed by police cars

The Weather Map

Nine bandits make £357,000 haul

Money made

No tax account

Horse falls on Lady Shawcross

'Doped' tyres

To-day's Text

Corn exchange plan

Better—dearer—cakes

Drivers have phones laid on

Body uncovered in garden of missing woman

POLICE, digging in the garden of Garden House, Routledge Buildings, Bedlington, East Northumberland late last night, found the body of a woman aged about 56.

Mrs. Lillian Crackett (56), who lives at Garden House, has been reported missing by Bedlington police by her brother, Mr. Joseph Allison, Pioneer Terrace, Bedlington Station.

INJURED SEAMAN LANDED

MAN DETAINED

POLICE WAITED

MILLIONS GONE

THE BEST YET

TRANSFERRED

Berlin tension rises again

From ANTONY TERRY

EAST-WEST tension here flared up to-night following the occupation by German police of part of a half-empty East Zone Railway H.Q. in the United States sector.

Independent Tory decides not to stand

COUNCILLOR H. M. HENDERSON, of Newcastle, last night decided not to stand as an Independent Conservative candidate for Newcastle North Division at the General Election.

CITY IMPROVES

SUPPORT US

Spain seeks Soviet wheat

SPAIN, faced with an acute food crisis, has now concluded an agreement for importing 300,000 tons of Russian wheat in exchange for oranges, according to business circles in Madrid.

Italian yards out of race

Smoky places may be photographed

No Nordic pact

Viscount (20) to follow family career

TWENTY - YEAR - OLD Viscount Furness, who is described as the richest boy in England — at 12 he inherited a large part of the £5,000,000 left to him by his father, the first Viscount Furness—is to make shipping his career.

Divina off Tyne to-day

THE Swedish tanker Divina, which was in collision with the submarine Truculent last Thursday, is expected off the Tyne piers at about 10 o'clock this morning.

Another walk-out at U.N. and Tokio

Tory College to shut till March

Resorts turn down invitation

Chess champion

Rejected Labour veteran refused peerage offer

MR. NEIL MACLEAN, the 74-year-old Govan (Glasgow) Socialist M.P., refused an offer of a peerage to the Prime Minister.

Found wife, three children gassed

Jet test flight

LATEST

'Britain on the brink'— bankers

FROM OUR CITY EDITOR

TWO of our leading bankers, Lord Balfour of Burleigh, chairman of Lloyds Bank, and Captain Eric Bowater, National Provincial chief, at charges of more than £2,000,000,000 of the public's money which the country is on the brink of financial disaster.

19 January, 1950.

7

the French Prime Minister, Guy Mollet, sought a meeting with the British Prime Minister, Sir Anthony Eden, to discuss the possibility of a union of the two countries with Her Majesty the Queen becoming Head of State of both countries. This proposal was rejected by Eden, although he was not averse to greater co-operation with France. The foundation of the European Union was also laid down during this decade with the formation of the European Economic Community. The launch of the Soviet satellite Sputnik heralded the space age, and NASA was founded in the United States in 1958. The jet age began with passenger flights by Comet and later, the Boeing 707. The late 1950s saw the start of a great change in the African continent with many countries gaining independence, leading to Sir Harold Macmillan's famous 'The wind of change is blowing over Africa' speech in 1960.

Many items with which we are now familiar and upon which we depend made their first appearances in the Fifties. The first year of the decade saw the introduction of the first modern credit card, Diners Club, in New York. On 25 June, the CBS Network

Sea cadets hold up the traffic on Northumberland Street, October 1952, as a car edges out of Prudhoe Street to join the trams and motor buses going south.

broadcast the first colour television programme, even though only a handful of sets could receive it. Colour receivers did not become generally available in the States until three years later. Other inventions in 1951 included super glue and power steering, and American disc jockey Alan Freed coined the term 'rock and roll'. That year saw the first commercial computer, a number crunching machine by Remington Rand called UNIVAC. In 1952 Mother Teresa opened her Home for Dying Destitutes in Calcutta. DNA was discovered in 1953 and the Black Box Flight Recorder was also invented. The first non-stick pan came in 1954 as did the trials of the first contraceptive pill. The first pocket-sized transistor radio was invented in Japan by the company now known as Sony, in 1955. Velcro, hovercraft and the TV remote control all appeared in 1956. The first commercial photocopier was introduced by Xerox in 1959.

A decade, then, of great innovation and change that surely was the start of the modern age in which we now live. It was certainly a great decade in which to grow up – sometimes frightening, sometimes hopeful, sometimes wondrous, but always fascinating and interesting.

From the 1956 official Newcastle guide.

... and in Newcastle upon Tyne

Like the rest of the world, Newcastle's 1950s began in post-war austerity but by the end of the decade we were in the 'never had it so good' society, according to Prime Minister Harold Macmillan. Although fuel rationing ended in 1950, other items, including many food items remained on ration: the era of rationing did not end completely until 1954. For the Coronation in 1953, everyone was allowed an extra pound of sugar and four ounces of margarine!

In Newcastle the decade got off to an interesting, if unusual, start when on 23 January there was a visit from Mr F.B. Thomas, mayor of the cattle town of Newcastle, Wyoming, who promptly granted honorary citizenship of his home town to every resident of our city!

In an attempt to cheer up the population, and to celebrate the centenary of the Great Exhibition of 1851, the government promoted the Festival of Britain in 1951. Although the main events were held in London, regional centres also participated and in Newcastle special events were held for two weeks from 29 May at Exhibition Park, the Stephenson Wing at King's College, and the Municipal Museum of Science and Engineering. A replica of the main South Bank Exhibition in London was on display on board the Festival Ship, HMS *Campania*, moored at the Quayside. The Festival of Britain created a demand for new fashions in furniture and furnishings including new styles of pottery, ceramics, and fabrics as well as furniture made from revolutionary materials such as fibreglass, plywood, formica and plastics.

Television started here in May 1953 when a temporary transmitter at Pontop Pike, near Anfield Plain, was brought into service so that people in this area could watch the Coronation before the main station came into operation later in the year. Although Independent Television began in London in 1955, we had to wait until 1959 when Tyne Tees Television was awarded the franchise for providing programmes in our region.

Several Royal visits to the region took place in the 1950s, beginning in April 1950 when Princess Margaret launched the 28,000-ton oil tanker *Velutina* at Wallsend, the largest vessel of its kind to be built in this country. Following the death of King George VI on 6 February 1952, the accession of Queen Elizabeth II was proclaimed in front of 3,000 people in St Nicholas Square two days later. Her Majesty the Queen and HRH the Duke of Edinburgh visited on 29 October 1954. In July 1956, Her Majesty Queen Elizabeth the Queen Mother attended the Royal Agricultural Show at the Town Moor. There was a record four-day attendance of

HMS *Campania* moored just below the Ouseburn on a busy River Tyne, 1951.
Opposite, the launch of *Velutina* from the Swan Hunter yard at Wallsend, April 1950.

more than 242, 000 visitors. The Queen Mother visited again on 31 October that year to officially open the new premises of Rutherford Grammar School on the West Road. The new premises of its sister school, Rutherford High School on Grange Road, were opened by Princess Margaret on 30 April 1959.

The Coronation of the Queen on 2 June 1953 was an occasion of great pride and joy. Four days earlier, the Coronation decorations in the streets were officially inaugurated and some buses were specially adorned. On the day itself, sadly, all outdoor celebrations had to be cancelled because of pounding rain, but people just moved their street parties indoors to homes or church halls. The week's programme included music and dancing in the parks, concerts, a bonfire and fireworks on Town Moor, and the Lord Mayor's Show and Procession on the Saturday.

The most noteworthy sporting events were probably the three FA Cup wins by Newcastle United. On 28 April 1951 they beat Blackpool 2-0. Between 200,000 and 250,000 spectators lined the streets for the team's celebration drive through the city with skipper Joe Harvey holding the cup aloft. One year later, on 3 May, the team beat Arsenal 1-0 for their second successive win. Then three years later, the winning score against Manchester City was 3-1.

Newcastle Airport was also thriving during this decade. The first post-war air link to the continent was inaugurated on 20 June 1950 with a flight to Geneva. A new air service to London began on 15 May 1953 by Hunting Air Transport. The first turbo-prop Viscount aircraft to land at Newcastle Airport landed on 31 May 1955, 61 minutes after leaving London with a full complement of 54 passengers. BKS Air Transport launched its inaugural flight to Scandinavia on 4 June 1958 with a flight to Bergen.

Some other Newcastle 'firsts' during the 1950s included:

- The first Mobile Library (right), 1 November 1950.
- Exhibition Park Model Railway, 12 May 1951.
- The City twinning with Nancy in France, 11 August 1954.
- The Municipal Stadium built on Ouseburn Tip used for the first time, 11 June 1955.
- Slatyford Transport Depot opened, 10 July 1956.
- The Majestic Ballroom – the former Gaumont Cinema – opened, 26 February 1959.
- Kenton Library opened, 9 September 1959.
- John Marley School officially opened, 9 December 1959.
- The Shieldfield Redevelopment Scheme inaugurated, 11 December 1959.

A church outing to Melrose from St Michael's in the west end of Newcastle, summer 1952.

It cost us nothing, the buses picked us up, two 44-seaters. I was 14 and I remember getting that checked coat. It was pale turquoise blue. We were all well dressed. There weren't many private households but you could eat your food off the steps they were that clean. You could bring your children and grand children on the trips and we had them every year. My granddad, who was on the committee, organised them. My grandma is next to me.

Mary McArdle (second row from the back, third from the right)

Foreign holidays were unusual, and much of the population enjoyed annual breaks at holiday camps in places like Filey. Days out were spent in the city centre's Leazes and Exhibition Parks (where we fished for tiddlers in the lakes and listened to the bands) and in the many local parks or at the seaside. We would travel to Whitley Bay, Tynemouth and Cullercoats, my favourite, either on the electric trains with their splendid bucket seats, or on the United bus. Trips were also made to South Shields and Seaburn or Roker on the train.

Exhibition Park lake in the early 1950s. The bridge had been built over the lake as a route to the Museum of Science and Engineering but was later removed.

Only 33 per cent of households had washing machines, even fewer households (15 per cent) had access to fridges or freezers and tumble dryers were extremely rare. Only ten per cent of households possessed a telephone, and many of those that did used a party line where the number was shared with another subscriber. Most food shopping was done on a daily basis using local shops. Only a handful of shops were self-service; the first of these was introduced by Sainsbury's in Croydon in 1950. Car ownership, however, more than doubled during the decade. A new Standard car cost £624 9s 2d. I wonder where the tuppence came from? A spring interior mattress cost £2 10s. A packet of Farley's Rusks would set you back 9d (about 4p) and a packet of ten Park Drive cigarettes 1s 3d. In 1958, a 17 inch TV set could be bought for 67 guineas or rented for 11 shillings per week. A Baby Belling cooker cost £43 19s and a steam dry iron £4 12s 1d (there's that odd penny again).

Newcastle was a thriving regional capital, as it is now, and boasted several large department stores. Fenwick's was where it still is in Northumberland Street. Adjoining stores in Market Street were Bainbridge and Binns. Bainbridge became part of the John Lewis chain in the 1950s and relocated in the 1970s to premises in the Eldon Square shopping precinct. Binns sadly is no longer with us. J. T. Parrish on Shields Road in Byker was very popular with shoppers from all over the city and was easily accessible by the excellent public transport provided by Newcastle Corporation. There was also Rowland Blaylock in New Bridge Street and a store on Scotswood Road near the junction with Park Road, called Dodds. A Boots branch on Northumberland Street, with its distinctive architecture, had a narrow wooden escalator, one of the earliest in the city. The fine Co-op building housing the main Co-op store in the city was also a great attraction for shoppers. There were two city centre branches of Woolworth, one in Northumberland Street and one in Clayton Street. The main music store was J.G. Windows in Central Arcade where I bought my first records which were, of course, 78 rpm discs. Happily, the shop is still there.

Newcastle's Official Guide for 1956 displays Bainbridge's Progress Report as part of the John Lewis empire. Binns had become part of the House of Fraser empire in 1953.

Progress Report

OUR determination to march with the times and present new ideas and vitality in both merchandise and store design has brought us many extra customers and much local renown.

We like to feel that in our Store you will find maximum shopping comfort, a friendly atmosphere and always something suited to your taste and pocket. Do pay us a visit.

Open all day Saturday. Closed for half-day Wednesday: 1 p.m.

BAINBRIDGES

BAINBRIDGE & CO. LTD., NEWCASTLE UPON TYNE 1
A Branch of The John Lewis Partnership

Old Eldon Square was, like today, a favourite summer relaxation spot for shoppers and workers.

After over a century of heavy industry, the fine architectural features of the Newcastle streets were black with soot and grime, and even warm, strong sunshine could not cheer them up. On cold and miserable days, the bright yellow buses were sometimes the only sign of cheer in the streets. However, following the passing of the Clean Air Act in 1956, a decision was taken to clean them up, and in the following decades this work was carried out fastidiously so that the fine Georgian and Victorian buildings are once again seen in all their glory.

Growing up in Newcastle in the 1950s was splendid and I wouldn't have missed it for the world. The city, the country and the world experienced a great deal of change, as did I, moving from childhood to teenager, and from the world of schoolboy to the world of work. It was a brilliant decade, which laid the foundations for the Swinging Sixties. I did not enjoy them half as much as the Fifties – maybe because I was older and gaining responsibilities. There was an atmosphere of friendship and caring and neighbourliness in the Fifties. Life then seemed more leisurely and less frantic than in later decades. Or maybe it's just remembering the sunny days rather than the rainy days. I suppose that's what is called nostalgia!

Douglas Bond

No, the weather wasn't all good in the 1950s.

Snow clearing on Northumberland Street in January 1955. This type of machine can't have been very successful as it did not survive. The shop on the corner of Lisle Street was Thomas Hunter's needlework depot.

The 65 bus on its way from Stamfordham Road to Forest Hall, 1958. It is travelling east along Blackett Street with Gallowgate in the background. This bus was No. 176, an AEC Regent V, one of 40 in the Newcastle Corporation Transport fleet.

Memories are Made of This

Dean Martin, 1955

A 1950s childhood

A Blakelaw boyhood

I was born in 1950 and lived in a prefab on Binswood Avenue, Blakelaw (with my brother, Mam and Dad) until the age of nine. I remember it as a peaceful area.

There was no playground nearby, so kids spent a lot of time on the streets, where we played kick the can, 'Japs and English' or Cowboys and Indians. We made a lot of our own toys – bows and arrows, catapults with thick elastic, and go karts. Sometimes we played in a derelict bunker on Slatyford Road. I remember it being flooded. There were a few very large trees on our street that were good for climbing. Indoors we played with our Dinky toys and made model warships. We didn't have a television or many books other than encyclopedias but we had lots of comics – *Topper*, *Dandy* and *Beano*.

Carl Gustafson

Carl and elder brother Keith outside the prefab on Binswood Avenue around 1954.

Although we didn't have much I could see that I wasn't the poorest kid in my class. My mother made great wholesome food with lots of local vegetables, and we kept hens (for eggs) in the back garden.

The prefab was comfortable with a coal fire but of course it was before the days of modern household appliances. My mother

The shelter at Nuns Moor Park, early 1950s.

used a poss tub filled with hot water and a poss stick to wash our clothes.

I learned to swim at Fenham baths where hygiene couldn't have been the highest priority. I remember we once took in an inflated lorry inner tube we had found on the street.

Weekends were often spent at Tamworth Road in the West End visiting my dad's family, or in Spital Tongues with my mother's brothers and sisters (all six of them). We played at Nuns Moor playground where there were swings and roundabouts and watched the old men playing bowls.

Saturdays were 'busy'. There was fish n'chips at Robinson's on Stanhope Street and the Saturday matinee at the Brighton picture house on Westgate Road. We took the trolley bus into Newcastle where we often went to the Green Market. There was also Milburn's seafood bar on Percy Street where for sixpence you could get a plate of mussels or cockles.

I loved visiting the terrace house on Tamworth Road with the family telling

stories around the coal fire (my dad was a great storyteller) and sliding down the banister into the back yard where the toilet was.

In the downstairs flat lived Jimmy Temple, a real character – he had a huge collection of cigarette cards in pristine condition. He also collected medals, which he displayed in his barber shop on Stanhope Street. Everybody seemed to collect something (some still do) – beer mats, insects, labels from bottles and stamps. Of course the 'ultimate' collection was at the Hancock Museum. I remember in particular the large collection of stuffed birds.

At the Central Station we enjoyed train spotting (they were steam trains). Among others we saw Mallard and The Flying Scotsman; they seemed to be always clean and well polished.

In the late 50s we got our first car, a Riley Adelphi. It had beautiful blue leather seats. The Riley gave us access to Sunday trips into the Northumberland countryside and also transport for our summer holiday, usually at Budle Bay up the coast. We loved the beaches there, collecting shells and playing in the sand dunes. Once we found a skeleton washed up on the beach.

A vending machine at the Central Station, 7 October 1954. It was the end of sweet rationing.

One of my last memories of the 1950s was when our relatives from Sweden came to visit us. They came on the ferry from Gothenburg to the Tyne. My Uncle Arne (Arne Gadd) was a gifted watercolourist and he used the Newcastle docks and boats in his paintings. It was fascinating for me to

The 'diamond crossing' at Newcastle Central Station, 1955. A steam train bound for Edinburgh chugs north while one of the green electric trains that operated on the coastal route waits at the platform.

watch him drawing and painting on the Quayside while I sat in the back of our parked car.

At Tamworth Road the first Indian families were moving in – funny, they painted their houses on the outside, and as we would all find out, they knew how to make great food. In 1959 we moved out of the city to Heddon-on-the-Wall. The Sixties were on the way.

Carl Gustafson

A stroll under one of the giant mobile cranes on Newcastle Quayside. This looks like a quiet weekend.

Terry Quinn

A family picnic in Elswick Park, late 1950s. It was unusual to see Indian families in the city at the time, but they would soon become a vibrant part of local culture.

22

Back Lanes in Byker

My playground wasn't a grassed area or lawn (they didn't exist in the locality) but a gas-lit lane with 8ft brick walls on either side. There were no Health and Safety concerns in those days and nothing to prevent us from walking, or even running, along them. No one fell, perhaps because we knew it was dangerous and learned to take care of ourselves, something lost in today's safety conscious culture. There was no prohibition on bangers on bonnie night, though the girls

Joe (centre) with younger brother Nicholas on the left and pal Ronnie in the back lane of Parker Street Byker around 1959.

did not take to kindly to having them being chucked in their direction, no one to stop you having a bonfire with what ever you could pinch from the neighbouring enemy lanes, which even in the next street seemed a world away. What real harm was done when a few back doors were scorched with the heat?

Why go to a park to play where you might have to run far when a 'cassie' (football) was kicked too hard, when you could play 'doors'? Playing this way meant that everyone had their own goal (the back door), the only arguments arose if the door was closed and it wasn't clear whether the ball had hit it! The ensuing debate was always won by the biggest or the best fighter.

Why play hide and seek in a park when you could climb into someone's back yard (not the one with the Alsatian in it though) and hide in an air raid shelter (dark and dank though it may be) where you'll never be found? As far as playing 'liggies' (marbles) is concerned, then grass is a non-starter.

In the summer cricket was the game, as long as we could borrow a dustbin for a wicket. It wasn't without risks – being hit by a tennis ball did not hurt but the reaction of Meggie Rickards, one of the neighbours, when a ball broke her window certainly did.

Where but in a back lane would you get ice cream from Quadrini's van provided it was not a washing day and it could negotiate the washing lines strewn across the lane? Where else could you get a ride on a fancy horse-drawn cart for a penny, or to hear the junk man on his horse and cart shouting for scrap?

Joe Rogerson

In nearby Walker there was a man who came round with a pony and trap and a small monkey that used to sit on the back of the trap. If your parents gave you a penny you could go for a ride round the streets. For more money you were allowed to hold the monkey and have your picture taken. Unfortunately this monkey bit my brother on the

Kendal Street, Byker.

Elspeth Rutter

Washday, Heaton, around 1958. The washing was snapped by camera-happy students from the nearby outpost of Newcastle College of Art.

side of the hand. He had to spend the night in hospital as it became very swollen. As this wasn't the first time the monkey had bitten, the police stopped the man from taking it in his cart.

Horse and carts were a common sight as there weren't many private cars. The coal man, milk man, rag and bone man and the drayman all used carts. It wasn't uncommon for people to move house using a horse and cart; it would be a funny sight now to see wardrobes, beds, and chairs piled on the back of a cart. The knife sharpener came round regularly on his bicycle and for a few pence he would sharpen any blades you had.

Before TV you amused yourselves by playing games such as snakes and ladders. Jigsaws were very popular because the

These hawkers with their caravan were caught on camera in a back lane near Scotswood Road in April 1957 by Tyneside photographer Jimmy Forsyth.

whole of the family helped. Summertime was great because you could play out with all your friends. If you had a ball you were everyone's friend as so many games involved one. Two teams, one either side of the street, and a tin can and a ball kept you amused for a while. Butter fingers and tag, top and whip, marbles, skipping ropes (great for Cowboys and Indians to tie people to lamp posts) rounders and a piece of chalk – happy days! Anyone who had an old pram to get rid of was popular because you could make your bogie with the pram wheels and any old bits of wood your dad had lying around. With a piece of rope tied to the front wheels you were away, though your shoes usually ended up taking a bashing as the bogie didn't have any brakes.

Pat Rogerson

Top left, Paddy Freeman's park, early 1950s, on the 'witch's hat' after sailing a home-made yacht in the pond.

Right. Pat and her brother and friends on a trip to London around 1958. Possibly this was before the unfortunate monkey bite incident in Newcastle (see page 25)!

Playing out and in

I was eight in 1960 when we moved from Scarborough Road, so Byker was my playground in my early years. I played football on the bowling green in Byker Park (when the 'parkie' wasn't around) and cricket on the waste ground at the top of Scarborough Road and Benson Road with my mates David Hartridge, Gordon Nicol, Ronnie Duncan and Duncan Bracken. Young boys joining in with the older boys was a dangerous combination, which is probably why I was hit on the nose by a cricket ball. I only suffered a nose bleed.

We usually raced our bogies on the Quarry on Union Road where B&Q is now situated. One day I managed to get all the way to the ferry landing near the 'glue factory' at the bottom of Welbeck Road. It was a long way back home, pulling my bogie uphill!

Tony Nixon

Photos: Hazel Nixon

Right, my brother Tony and me with Mum holding the new arrival, our brother Keith, in Heaton Park. We would have walked from Scarborough Road in Byker and back. A long way for little legs! Above, Tony and me with Keith in his Silver Cross pram. We were very well behaved and never let go of the pram handles while walking next to Mum.

Hazel Nixon

If this photograph from 1959 was taken on a Saturday we would be watching William Tell or Hawkeye. If on a Sunday, Lassie, Robin Hood or Sunday Night at the London Palladium. Hazel Nixon

How much is that kitty in the window? Window shopping around 1955.

Bumps and hopscotch

In the summer the streets were teeming with children of all ages; the older ones looked out for the little ones. There seemed to be more girls than boys in our area so if the boys wanted to play football or cricket they had no choice but to include the girls, not that I was any good. The older girls would organise games of rounders and everyone was included. Fairless Street [Byker] was quite a wide street and there were few cars; in all the games we played, we never broke a window. We also played with a huge skipping rope that stretched the width of the street and everyone joined in. My brother Stephen became quite proficient, as did all the boys. We younger girls were in awe of the older girls who could play The Bumps. The skipping rope was turned very fast and the skipper had to concentrate and skip at the right time or they ended up with weals on the back of their legs from the rope.

We played jacks, two ballers and hopscotch. My Nana would insist we swilled the path when we had finished our game and we would have to draw another hopscotch grid the next day if we wanted to play.

My brother and I were given large three-wheeler bikes one Christmas and we played for hours up and down the street until I hit the kerb and went over the handle bars. I split my lip and grazed my hands and legs. In those days you didn't rush to A&E. There was a neighbour who lived in our street who was a member of the St John's Ambulance Brigade – all the children were taken to his house to be patched up. I can remember him giving me a sweet to stop me crying and I got away with a fat lip, cuts and bruises.

I can not remember ever being indoors during the summer months and even in winter we played outdoors (though quite often we came in to warm up). My Granda Lewens was very good at woodwork and he made us a sledge out of scrap wood with shaped metal runners. My brother spent hours playing on it but after one go I preferred to stay in doors. I never did like the snow. Granda also made me a

I am sitting on our television in my Sunday best. The photograph was taken by a photographer who would go around the streets knocking on doors and taking snaps of families. The dress was lilac chiffon and as soon as the photographer left it was taken off and hung up and I was put back into my old clothes to play in the street.

dolls' house. It was amazing with lights in every room. There was a battery concealed in the roof space powering tiny torch bulbs. The rooms were decorated with wallpaper and it had curtains at the windows. He even made the furniture. He also made Stephen a fort with turrets and a mechanical drawbridge. I don't know how he did it without us finding out as we were always at our grandparents'. As young as we were, we appreciated the fact he had spent so much time making our presents and had hours of fun playing with them.

In the warm weather young mums would leave their babies at the front door to get some fresh air. The older girls would knock and ask 'can I take your baby for a walk?' There would be lines of girls walking up and down the street pushing beautiful high prams.

The 1950s were a great time to grow up as we could play outdoors without our parents worrying. We never strayed from the front street, and made many lasting friendships.

Lynn Steele

Lynn Steele

Our backyard on a hot summer's day. The little dark haired boy is my brother Stephen and the little blonde boy was Michael Dawson who lived up-stairs. Even with short hair I had to have a huge ribbon in my hair!

Windy warmers

We all made windy warmers on very cold nights. A 'windy warmer' consisted of a tin – the large size for powdered baby milk. Two holes were punched in the sides near the top and wire or string threaded through these to make a long handle. The tin was filled with sticks and paper, later small coals; the bottom had holes for air circulation. The whole creation swung in the black night air as we twirled them in arcs about us, hot sparks flying, unaware that those of us who used string and not wire ran the risk of incinerating their neighbours. The harder they swung the redder they roared and from time to time we set them down and warmed our hands. 'Windy warmers' ushered in that change of seasons when summer frocks became winter ones, not by a change of wardrobe, but by the addition of a cardigan knitted by my grandmother. Added to this outfit were grey ribbed woollen stockings. Mother would never invest in suspenders, so we wore torturous home-made elastic garters that had to be tight enough to hold up stockings through our very active days. In doing so, the garters cut off almost all of our circulation. It still amazes me that a large percentage of female Geordies aren't amputees. At bedtime we had great purple and red weals grooved into our thighs and we cursed mother's economy.

The other source of conflagration was November 5th, 'Guy Fawkes Night'. Months before it was talked of; weeks before it was saved for. Not money, but old paper, cardboard and furniture. Mothers with poor control over their children had to be watchful of their chairs and tables or they might find themselves walking into bare rooms. There were numerous raids on back yards that had their doors inadvertently left open; whole suites of old furniture moved from one territory to another with accusations of 'cheat' and 'thief' filling the air. The neighbourhood was too respectable for gang warfare.

Sofas burned best; the burning of the heavy wood was slowed down by the padding, so that they burned for a long time. One of father's few extravagances was to supply us with fireworks. These were lit after dark on Guy Fawkes' Night after the bonfire was lit and before 'the pub'. Father always bought them at Norman Long's, his newsagent and fellow Brown Ale drinker. My favourites were the Roman Candles, incandescent flowing gold, and Catherine Wheels. Father nailed the latter to the back yard door instead of pinning it. This slowed the wheel down, so that when at last it was burned out, so was the back door paint. We must have been the only house in the street with a back door re-painted every year; and us only tenants!

We all stayed up half the night, which was probably only until eleven o'clock. When the bonfire died down, the boys put potatoes in the embers to bake and if we were lucky we were allowed to share. Each street had its own bonfire and everyone declared next day that theirs had been the biggest and the best; at least six imaginary feet taller than the nearest rival. Strength was added to the argument if, on the way to school next day, the embers of 'your' fire were still red. The fire brigade was out most of the night correcting small errors of judgement with large amounts of water and the local hospital had an annual boom not unlike the Klondike gold rush.

Patricia Bensdorp Clark

Growing up in Throckley

My childhood in mid 1950s Throckley, now part of Newcastle, was rather different to being brought up in a city. We were right on the edge of the town and just up the road were green fields and open countryside. In the summer we fished for sticklebacks in Throckley Dene and in winter we sledged down 'Jonnas Bank' almost into the stream itself. Summer games included cricket and in the winter we kicked a football or tennis ball around. The Miners' Welfare Ground was just up the road and some of us played tennis and bowls in the endless summers. We were outdoors all the time, playing games or riding our bikes.

The Lyric, Throckley, before 1963.

There were no televisions or cars – we were all as poor as each other on the council estate. It was the age of the cinema and ours was the Lyric, which had three showings every week and a children's matinee on Saturday morning.

The Throckley Co-op provided all we wanted for everyday life. Every week the order man came and listed all the groceries we needed on a long order form; a couple of days later the goods were delivered. Sometimes we went down to the Co-op and it was endlessly fascinating for a little boy to watch the pneumatic-fired balls rolling along their guide tracks to the office and coming back with the correct change. Regular purchases were mantles for the gas lighting; we had electricity but gas was cheaper. Once, but only once, I touched the fragile globe to see what happened –the result was a broken mantle and a telling off.

A special treat was a visit to 'the Town' for shopping, or, even more special, en route to the sea-side. Newcastle seemed huge and so busy. The Grainger Market and Green Market were so crowded a little boy could easily be swept away, or so it seemed. Eating out was almost unknown, and restaurants only for the better off, but as a special treat I would be taken to Bowers cafe in Nuns Lane for fish and chips.

David Rochester

Bowers Restaurant

NUNS LANE, NEWCASTLE

Parties Catered For

The North East's Foremost Fish Caterers

8,000 Satisfied Customers each week

Established 1925

Bowers Restaurants (N/c) Ltd.   PHONE 2-6909

This submarine, with queues of small boys, was photographed on the Quayside by Jimmy Forsyth around 1957.

Bowers fish and chips restaurant was unusual in that you stood in a queue by a little kiosk inside the entrance on the ground floor, ordered your meal and paid for it there, receiving a small number of tickets as required to hand over upstairs in exchange for your meal. The fish and chips were very good though we never went more than once a week. It was a treat! Brian Fagleman

I was taken to visit a submarine moored on the Quayside one afternoon for an exciting treat. You could be taken round the terrifyingly claustrophobic interior. I became very scared that we'd never escape, and had to be hauled out in hysterics by a very unsympathetic sailor against the one way flow of visitors. It was no treat! Anna Flowers

Over the river from Gateshead

I was born on May 6th, 1947 in Bensham, Gateshead. I remember walking across Redheugh Bridge to Wengers to buy clothes courtesy of a loan from the 'Provi'. The yellow trams always used to fascinate me as we only had buses in Gateshead. We would get the 53 Saltwell Road bus home from near the Central Station. We stood for what seemed like hours waiting for the bus to arrive and I spent most of that time keeping an eye on the statues, giant men or angels wrapped in robes sitting around, staring into the distance and ignoring each other. They are still there, opposite the entrance to the Royal Station Hotel.

Jimmy Forsyth snapped the Stephenson Monument around 1957.

We also used to go to a pantomime every year at the Empire, our seats were always up in the 'gods', I still have dreams about walking up the almost vertical stairs.

My happiest memory was when my mam, brother and I had just passed the Hancock Museum on our way to the circus on the Town Moor. I was walking on a low wall which I loved doing. We were overtaken by a troupe of elephants and their trainers walking slowly along the main road, I jumped off the wall and walked alongside them for what seemed like an age when suddenly a baby elephant stole my hat. It was thrilling and I haven't forgotten it.

Vera Rooke

Sunday Quayside

We used to walk along the banks of the Tyne on Sunday, crossing the Swing Bridge to be entertained by the men selling dinner services from their stalls on the quayside. We would take the lift to the road level of the Tyne Bridge and walk back to the Gateshead side. Did we then get a bus home? I honestly can't remember.

Vera Rooke

A visit to the Quayside on Sundays was to partake of a glass of sarsaparilla and watch the jumping beans men – in those days there were no railings to prevent falls into the river and no fancy buildings either with much of the frontage being taken by derelict warehouse sheds.

Joe Rogerson

The Quayside Sunday Market, 1955.

Easter

Easter was salmon, in tins, pink, from Canada. Father only ate it with boiled new potatoes and cucumber in vinegar, no other salad, despite mother's encouragement to try it; rabbit food he called it. We always went to church on Good Friday and Easter Sunday and if father was with us, which in itself was a rarity, we had to do something 'different' on the way home. I remember the year we all climbed Grey's Monument, honouring the reformer, 165 steps or so, an exhausting upwards spiral towards Earl Grey on his plinth and a tiny parapet from which the whole world swayed below. It was there my sister, chalk white, discovered a fear of heights and almost vomited on the crowds below. It was certainly value for money – for fourpence we were all thoroughly shaken. We went home to our pink salmon tea after which we went out into the lane to play cricket and my sister Meg got hit in the face with a cricket-bat. It all gave the day a little more variety than we were accustomed to.

Patricia Bensdorp Clark

Birthday treats

My birthday treat was to choose a small cake from Smythe's cake shop in Newcastle. The shop assistants all wore black with white aprons and little white caps and the cakes were like nothing else you'd seen before.

Pat Rogerson

The view from Grey's Monument, 1957 captured by Jimmy Forsyth. The Clean Air Act had been passed in 1956 and all those chimneys (well, not quite all) were now smokeless.

Christmas treats

I'd had tea and was playing with my dolls when my grandfather came home from work. 'Come on,' he said, 'Put your hat and coat on. We're going out'. Despite all my pleadings, he wouldn't tell me where. The most I could get out of him was that we were 'going to see the lights'. I couldn't see the sense of this. It was winter, so it was cold, dark and I could look out of the window and see a line of street lights. These stretched around the crescent where I lived with Mam, Dad, Nana and Granad (as I called him). It was around seven years after the end of the World War 2 and I was four years old.

Mam and Dad must have been out somewhere, because I can't remember them being there to say goodbye as I skipped off between my grandparents. I was so excited. I don't remember ever going out in the dark before that, and there we were getting on a tramcar and heading off to the big city. The tram stopped outside the Central Station and went in to see the huge decorated Christmas tree, given by the

people of Norway to the people of Newcastle as a thank you for their support during the war. The bottom of the tree was surrounded by a wire fence. Inside this were wrapped gifts, donated by people for poor children.

The noisy station with its snorting steam trains, whistling guards, yelling newspaper vendors, and bustling travellers was thrilling, but the best was yet to come. We joined the throng of people heading towards the shopping streets.

I began to understand. Brightly coloured lights were strung along the route. The big shops – Binns, Bainbridge's and Fenwick's had fantastic Christmas themed windows, displaying toys, party clothes and beautiful gifts. Best of all many windows featured animated fairy story scenes. The Prince bending over Sleeping Beauty to kiss her awake, the Seven Dwarves chipping away in their jewelled mine, Santa's workshop – his elves at work making toys, a magic sleigh drawn by Rudolf and his friends across a sparkling sky, and model trains stuffed with presents chugging round the track, through tunnels and over cotton wool covered mountains. It was truly fairy land.

After years of austerity it must have seemed as magical for the adults as it did for children.

Newcastle Central Station, early 1950s.

Opposite, a tram and a trolley bus in the snow outside the Central Station in 1947, just a few years earlier.

After seeing the Norwegian Christmas tree in the Central Station, I wanted to leave a gift under it for poor children. At home I put my ration of sweets and some little toys and books I had grown too old for in a shoe box. Mam helped me wrap the box in Christmas paper. A few days later we took the gift by tram to the Central Station. Stretching over the wire fence to put my present with the others that surrounded the huge tree, I hoped that the child who received my gift would be happy with it. As we walked away, I turned back for one last look and was shocked to see a man lean over the fence, pick up my gift and run off with it. At the time I was very upset, especially about the little girl or boy who would not get a present on Christmas day.

Now I like to think that the man gave the present to his own child. Perhaps he couldn't afford to buy anything himself. I hope it helped to make Christmas day happy for them.

Tana Durham

Christmas and New Year in the back lanes were social events with lots of to-ing and fro-ing, particularly at New Year. As there were no TVs, people made their own entertainment. Lots of baking and cooking was done on New Year's Eve ready for the 'first footers'. Because we had a piano the party tended to end at our house!

Christmas seemed to come round a lot more slowly than it does today, maybe because there was no TV showing toy adverts and the shops didn't start putting the Christmas items out straight after the summer holidays. Grandad came into his own at this time of year, which was the one time we were allowed to go to the club as he had paid for us to attend the Christmas party. Dads also had works Christmas parties. I remember going to Walkergate to attend a party for the railway men's children – it was the best ever! The presents were great and you were allowed to open them before Christmas as Santa gave them to us himself and said it was okay!

We made decorations for the living room ceiling; paper chains painstakingly made from coloured paper. These would be strung from corner to centre. Balloons were also suspended from the

The dog looks rather worried in this Christmas snap.

ceiling but these always looked very sad by New Year's Eve. Christmas trees were always tiny compared to today's giants and they were decorated with glass ornaments that were very fragile.

On Christmas Eve you went early to bed in your new pyjamas, after eating a fresh sweet mince pie that Mam had made. We always had a sixpence, a Jaffa orange, a shiny red apple and sometimes a hanky or a pair of mittens in our

Pat Rogerson

Pat and her twin brother, Peter, meet Father Christmas at the works party.

stocking. A game of some sort, ludo or snakes and ladders and a book were always wrapped up. If you read a particular comic then you got the annual. It was *Dandy* and *Beano* in our case, later to be replaced with *Bunty* and *Roy of the Rovers*. A small selection box and then the big present that you had asked Father Christmas for, one year a doll and pram, another a pair of roller skates that had a key that you could use to extend the length. Christmas dinner was usually at your grandparents'; chicken was a treat then.

Pat Rogerson

Christmas was 'chicken' when we were small. One year it was our very own; fattened and killed at a suitable moment by uncle Georgy, who was the only one who had the nerve. We sat on the kitchen table and watched in fascination and horror as the entrails were pulled out and the legs cut off. Without warning mother would pull on a sinew and make the amputated claw move and terrify us into thinking that it was still alive. I more than once fell off the table in an adrenaline rush of fright.

Christmas dinner was prepared after we got up a little late, having been to midnight mass. Father always delayed the progress and serving of the meal by coming home with an arrogant air and the smell of rum and peppermint, which he drank only in the festive season, on his breath. We never had a Christmas without a row.

After this we proceeded by tram to my grandma Clark's house. My father usually visited his mother just twice a year; Christmas and Easter. Here there was always a large colourful tea and some large decorated old ladies who spent their time playing Haymarket, a card game I could never follow as we were not encouraged to join in. After the delight of opening the gifts, Meg and I almost died of boredom. It took us years to realise that our parents had a private signal that meant that they got up and left for a drink at the pub and we were 'allowed' to sleep over at grandma's. Every time mother promised us we didn't have to stay and every time she broke her word. Grandma was delighted and we were imprisoned

In later years Father staggered home each and every Christmas with a turkey weighing a stone. It was his annual gift from the shipyard. Father no doubt found it much heavier as he came home via the pub and the unaccustomed Christmas ration of rum and pep, too many and too late. Customarily it was roasted slowly while we were away at midnight mass, to be eaten re-warmed with the trimmings for Christmas dinner – at lunch time.

Ma and Pa Clark were cold meat fans. Some days after Christmas my sister and I began to pillage the bird one evening when they were out. It fell from the kitchen bench, not in itself a disaster; but where it fell was! As the outside lavatory had few attractions in winter, we were the happy owners of pots under our beds. These, my mother should have emptied immediately but she reduced the trips to once a day. She deposited the contents, with the tea leaves and other noxious waste in a bucket under the scullery sink – lidless. Into this odorous and diverse melange the plump and unsuspecting bird toppled. Dumbfounded we washed it inside and out. No one could understand our reluctance to eat the fowl; and fortunately no health dramas occurred to expose us. I confessed about 30 years later; my mother's face was a picture.

Our Christmas tree was always minuscule. I don't know to this day if that was due to economy or whether it was because the tree always stood on a rather tall aspidistra stand. The tree bore silver balls and a small house with icing sugar windows and tiny barley-sugar twisted candles, which were never lit. Around the walls of the room at cornice height, hung coloured paper chains and folding paper bells which expanded and contracted again to go into the box when Christmas was deemed to be over.

Patricia Bensdorp Clark

The Co-operative Society's Newgate Street store advertises the Christmas Toy Fair and Grotto in 1950.

Summer treats

During the school holidays we went to Whitley Bay on the train and had picnics on the sand with jam sandwiches and a bottle of pop. We often had a ride on the 'Shuggy Boats' – they had nothing to do with water but were pram-shaped swings with seats at either end and a rope in the middle. To get the 'boat' to move you had to pull the rope (a bit like bell ringing) and the harder you pulled the higher and faster you went. There were always the lovely donkeys to ride on too.

Pat Rogerson

Above, and left, Whitley Bay beach.

Our journey to Cullercoats (above, considered the safest beach by our parents) began at Heaton Station with its unique smell of wood, smoke and diesel, its vending machine dispensing Sunmaid raisins (a favourite) and the sound we made running up and down the wooden ramps and bridges. Hazel Nixon

In the summer holidays we went to Cullercoats on the green electric train from West Jesmond, and to the icy cold outdoor pool at Tynemouth (right).

Another treat was crazy golf outside the Plaza above the Long Sands.

Anna Flowers

During the summer holidays a special treat was to go to the seaside, either Tynemouth or Whitley Bay on the electric train from the Central Station. Right at the start of the summer holidays I was almost sick with the excitement of going on our annual holiday – always to Blackpool – on the Primrose Bus service from Marlborough Crescent bus station.

David Rochester

The Plaza, above the Long Sands, 1950s. What were these people watching?

We went to the coast (never the beach or the seaside, always the coast) by the circular railway, where you could choose which way go. My grandmother used to say West Jesmond Goes Forth coming Back With Monk Seaton, a corruption of some of the names of the stations on the line. Jane Jantet

Summer Sundays always involved an outing somewhere whenever the weather was anything like decent. We usually had trips to the seaside, almost invariably Cullercoats in our case, as this was my mother's favourite. However, she was always quite adventurous, and sometimes we would actually cross the Tyne and go to South Shields, Seaburn or Roker. At other times, we would go inland to the 'countryside' to Ryton Willows, where our favourite pastime was hiding under a railway bridge when a steam-hauled (of course, as there was nothing else) train thundered over the top of us. Such fun! Another inland trip was to North Wylam for picnics on the banks of the Tyne. Sometimes, when money was tight (there were four of us children to be paid for), and the train fares could not be raised, we would go either to the local park (Hodgkin Park or Elswick Park) or to Leazes Park where we would fish for 'tiddlers' in the lake. In the summer, we children and my mother would go to the pub with our father, as the Benwell House Hotel had an outside verandah where we would sit with our lemonade.

Douglas Bond

Cullercoats around 1950. The Dove Marine Laboratory above the beach had a little aquarium.

These smart lads in their best suits were cub scouts celebrating a birthday party in Hodgkin Park, Elswick, riding on the 'witch's hat' and climbing the 'jungle gym', late 1950s.

Monkey's blood

Yes it was thick red sugared juice with some strawberry essence thrown in … but it made the old fashioned ice cream taste lovely … who remembers Rea's Ices? or Quadrini? or Sam Zair? I remember old Mr Quadrini coming around Burnt Houses with his horse and cart … and had a real shiny tub of their own recipe ice cream … this was in the early 50s … when you got a penny ice stick, a tuppenny cornet, a threepenny cornet, and a tanner sandwich! This was liberally sprayed with the 'monkey's blood' and sucked gleefully by us kids … what a treat every Sunday!

I remember later, him coming in an old bull nosed Austin van complete with his whistle blowing its sharp shrill sound … there were two holes cut into the floor where he could stand upright in the back to serve everyone … then it was ice lollys too plus the famous '99' got an airing … the original was two cornets filled with ice cream and a Cadbury's flake pushed into the top … then they were one shilling!

Mike Heaviside

Music, ice cream and fish and chips

I was born in 1954 and grew up in Fenham. The 1950s had started off with my late father, Barney McKay, being banned from driving for years after crashing a friend's car through the front window of Carrick's Restaurant in Grey Street, and all the way into the café, on Christmas Day. I guess I'm lucky to exist as dad wasn't wearing a safety belt. We didn't get a car for many years after that. My earliest musical memory, aged three, was being fascinated by the jukebox in Quadrini's tiny ice cream parlour on Two Ball Lonnen in Fenham, next to the Regal Cinema. My mum, June McKay (always a serious coffee addict) used to go in for a coffee fix while I fed endless threepenny bits into that jukebox in order to repeatedly sing along to the same record, *Diana* by Paul Anka, which was a UK chart hit in 1957. My singing greatly amused the senior Quadrini's who were friendly with my mum, lovely, salt-of-the-earth people. They had two sons, Vincent and Michael. Their ice cream was very tasty … but not quite as good as Rea's ice cream.

When I was five I discovered Rea's ice cream parlour not far from St James's Park, while roaming around Newcastle on my bicycle. In those days there was hardly any traffic on the roads and children were allowed out to play without adult supervision and ride the streets on their bikes. Unimaginable today. My friends and I even played cricket in the middle of the road in Fowberry Crescent, Fenham, moving out of the way for the 'rag and bone' man with his horse and cart and on the rare occasion when a car came along. We just had to watch out for Hannah who drove her mini at breakneck speed; she lived in Bolbec Road, Fenham and was married to Thomas, a *Chronicle* journalist who later handled PR for T. Dan Smith. Rea's ice cream store had a great jukebox, and a fruit machine. My idea of heaven was riding to Rea's on my bike and playing music on their jukebox while enjoying a 99.

Barry McKay age three in 1957, already showing signs of growing up fast, with his stylish and fashionable mother, June, in trendy Capri pants and boxy Chanel style jacket.

However the very best ice cream in Newcastle was always at Mark Toney's in their shop in the Grainger Arcade and their ice cream parlour on Percy Street. Occasionally, on Sundays, my dad would take me there specially, on the number 32 trolley bus from Fenham (we still didn't have a car) for the most delicious ever ice cream, served in a glass with strawberry sauce on top. I would ask for 'an ice cream with red stuff on.' The awfully posh Mark Toney daughter behind the counter would

say, 'Do you mean STROW-berry?' My mum also enjoyed their coffee. Once, my dad's friend, Dr Carr, drove me there for a treat in his Bugatti in which I threw up, not being used to riding in motor vehicles. This was the very same Bugatti famously discovered in his lock-up after he passed away which was auctioned in Paris for £3m in 2009.

Another fond memory from the 1950s is Bowers restaurant which was in a lane off Nun Street (where my grandmother, Rachel McKay used to take me for a fish and chips treat, followed by a trip to the Essoldo or the Haymarket cinema). Bowers was a firm favourite of mine; diners had first to buy tickets from a cinema-style box office for each menu item they required before entering.

Disaster struck for me when the Paletta coffee bar opened up opposite Fenwick's. My mum, then only in her 20s, loved the 'espresso bongo' style of the Paletta, which was in a basement. They didn't sell Italian ice cream! Then matters got even worse. My mum started dragging me off to Fenwick's for morning coffee; their ice cream was horrible, silly models walked about promoting fashion available for sale and a live band played boring music. Sometimes my mum even dragged me into Carricks café on Grainger Street, a historic Newcastle establishment but just not my scene.

Barry McKay

Barry's fashion-conscious mother, June, would have appreciated these beautiful drawings by Fenwick's fashion artist Kath Kidd (née Connell) who illustrated the latest creations for the French Salon. Kath's work regularly appeared in the local press throughout the 1950s.

It was like entering a shrine when you visited Fenwick's French Salon. Christine Luke

This picture was taken in the late 1950s and features four of my grandfather Antonio Marcantonio's children, from left to right Maria, Anita, Alberto and Angela with Angela's husband Alex and finally Anita's husband Ernie. They were all aunts and uncles of mine. The picture was taken at the bottom of Stepney Bank, Byker, just down from our factory at the time, where we had a garage for keeping the vans. The vans were a new venture in the 1950s and we built the fleet up to about 20 vans in the 1960s. We no longer have ice cream vans of our own. Nowadays nearly all ice cream vans are owner-drivers but we still supply quite a lot of them.

My father and aunts told me that in the Fifties our parlours were very popular in the evenings with young people and courting couples – Percy St certainly had a Fifties look with red cubicles, patterned formica tables and a juke-box. Even today we still get elderly people reminiscing to us about how they met and did their courting in our parlours in Percy St, Byker and Gateshead High Street.

Anthony Marcantonio

Hospitals and the baby blues

In 1959, I was pregnant with my second child. We lived in Provost Gardens, Benwell. When my contractions started, my husband Eric was working (we didn't have a car, anyway) so I had to make my own way to the General Hospital, West Road. As there wasn't a direct bus to the West Road from Benwell, I had to get a bus into the City Centre, and then another bus to the West Road. My friend and neighbour looked after my two-year-old daughter. We lived in a very tight-knit community, and we all helped each other. At this time, the normal practice was to have home births rather than a hospital delivery. With my first pregnancy in 1957, however, I developed complications and had to have a Caesarian. The doctors were worried that the same might happen with my second child so I was told to go into hospital for that delivery too.

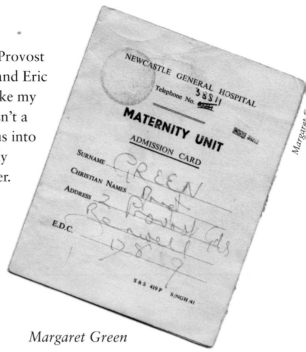

Margaret Green

The General Hospital, 1950.

I was born in 1947, the eldest of four children, and during the 1950s I gradually acquired two sisters and a brother. It was usual for women to give birth at home, attended by the district midwife, but our mother was convinced that new mothers needed a rest from domestic chores so chose to have her children in nursing homes where she could spend about two weeks apart from her family.

Our neighbour, the wife of the Medical Officer of Health for Newcastle, gave birth to twins at home and I was invited in to see the very new babies as part of my preparation for having a new brother or sister.

Shortly afterwards my sister was born in a nursing home in Gosforth. Children were not allowed to visit for fear of infection, but my grandmother misguidedly led me up a back lane so that I could look through a window to see the ward where my mother was confined. I have an abiding memory of a room full of beds with identical looking women in them. I couldn't tell which one was my mother, and was too young to understand directions such as left, right, or third bed. I panicked and became hysterical and had to be removed for fear of attracting attention. As I was dragged screaming back along the lane, my grandmother yanking my arm, a woman lent out of an upstairs window and asked what was wrong. This scene is very clear in my memory, and had a profound impact on my own decisions about where to have my children.

When my next sister was born in 1955, I was sent to stay with my paternal grandparents for a week or so. When my brother was born in 1959, I was aged 12, but was still considered too young to be allowed into the nursing home. Nevertheless, I went there on the bus with a friend, and we made our way into the upstairs room of Ashfield Nursing Home on Elswick Road, where we found my mother and my baby brother who was just a few hours old. The following day I went back again with a different friend, but was refused entry. My friend, who was 13, was told she could visit if she liked, because she was over the age barrier, although she didn't even know my mother. The next day I was due to go into hospital to have my tonsils removed, so I felt it was particularly cruel not to be allowed to see my mother. She leant out of the window to speak to me, but after that I didn't see her or my baby brother for another week.

Fiona Clarke

The children's ward

In 1958, when I was six, I was wrapped in a red blanket and rushed to the RVI by ambulance with appendicitis. Soon I was in an operating theatre under bright lights with the horrible black, evil smelling gas mask that I dreaded from visits to the dentist coming down over my face. Then there I was in a strange bed, in a strange nightie, feeling very ill and very scared. Parents weren't allowed outside of visiting hours, so I just screamed until my mum arrived (summoned early and from then allowed in at any time). After a few days it all got worse as I had contracted dysentery, so was moved into a side room, surely to the relief of everybody. The consultant visited us at home a few weeks later and told us that if the appendix hadn't been removed I would have died, so I felt rather important (and my mother was very grateful to the NHS).

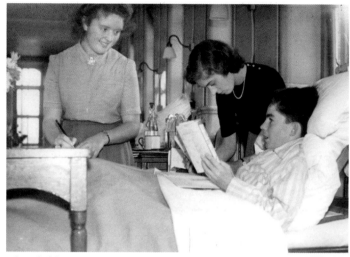

The children's ward at the RVI with hospital library staff, early 1950s.

When I had my tonsils out a year later at Walkergate Hospital I resolved to try to be good and not cry. I was still told off for making a fuss when my throat was very painful, which felt unjust as I was making an effort! I remember thick vegetable soup, jelly, and ice cream, and for some reason burnt, scratchy toast.

Anna Flowers

Polyphoto taken at Binns around 1956.

The broken home

In 1951 my father left home and, because my mother was entitled to 10 shillings a week support for me until I was sixteen years old, she had to go to the Magistrate's Court in Market Street to sign for and collect it. My mother had to work so there were many times, when I had to go and collect it. This I did not enjoy doing as nearly every week, after waiting in a long queue, I was informed that my father had not paid the maintenance.

Mary Dodds

School Day *(Ring Ring goes the Bell)*

Chuck Berry, 1957

Schoolboys and schoolgirls

Scholarship girl at the Sacred Heart

'The scholarship' loomed ahead. At school there was an inadequate attempt at coaching; some homework was given but not much, just fractions I remember and some compositions. Father helped our neighbour Margaret S. with arithmetic but rarely helped me. His argument was that I could do it myself, I wasn't stupid was I? At this time mother came to school for a talk with the teacher; no doubt other mothers came too, but standing next to mine, my teacher declared that Madeleine T. would pass the scholarship (she was bright) and Margaret S. but I had no hope. This outraged me because I knew that I was better at everything than Margaret and that the teacher was guilty of favouritism; the other two had slightly better clothing, elocution lessons in one case, but nothing else.

I had slight reservations about passing the scholarship, all because of a hat! My parents had promised in a moment of weakness that I could go to St Anne's if I didn't get the scholarship exam. There they wore a navy velour hat with a gold and blue band. At Fenham Convent I would have to wear a green beret with gold tassel and I hated the idea. St Anne's was not reputed to offer a good standard of education, but I didn't know that. It cost three and a half guineas per term and I don't think father would have kept me there after I was 16, but I had no understanding of the consequences of such a choice. I had even less knowledge of the fact that 'The Scholarship' was a key to the door of knowledge; that like Alice in Wonderland, once I opened it I would never be the same again. I remember walking in class-crocodile to get to the hall of another school to sit the exam. I must have had some natural wit, because what we learnt in those days at St Mary's, Rutherford Street, could have covered a postage stamp and still left space. One of the few historical facts we learnt was of the discovery of Tar McAdam, and we drew an ancient road in layers to illustrate this improvement.

One thing they were hot on was Irish dancing. Those girls whose parents paid for a velvet jacket, green skirt and shiny patent buckled shoes, were the privileged few. They went in for competitions and sometimes won silver medals. Mother would not or could not provide such items. Was snobbery a factor in deciding which children were suitable for such roles? They were probably influenced by economic considerations too. No doubt mother had an inkling of this, but of course I didn't. 'Not for the likes of us', was an often heard refrain, though not in our house. Many working class people in the Fifties still had a strong feeling of being expected to know their place and keep it.

Everyone waited with trepidation for the scholarship results. One Saturday morning, lying in bed, I heard my mother pick up the post in the passage (halls were posh); seconds later came a shout 'Ee our Jimmy, Patsy's passed the scholarship!'

Patricia is No. 3 in the back row of her class of 36 at the Sacred Heart, 1951.

Once mother had told half of Newcastle that our Patsy had passed, she set about complaining of the costs and sacrifices it entailed. In preparation for the heady world of the Sacred Heart Convent, we had to have the school uniform. The official school outfitter in the town (we always went to The Town despite Newcastle's city status), Raymond Barnes, would provide this at a price. Green blazer, woollen gym-slip and green knickers, with elastic in the legs, which stopped just above the knee. The gym-slip, a sort of sack with a braid belt, was worn in the first two years, decidedly a Twenties not Fifties cut. In addition a green tie and a cream blouse, out-door shoes, in-door sandals and gym shoes ('sand shoes' to us) for exercise of all kinds. Three pairs of shoes! An unheard of luxury. Glowing on the blazer in real gold thread was The Sacred Heart of Jesus. Despite my aversion to it, I was to wear the hated green beret with gold tassel. The clothing list was rounded off with a green Burberry coat and knitted scarf; in my case a more than adequately long one.

A clash of wills accompanied the purchase of a tennis racket at the Co-op. Here all significant purchases were made and a dividend of two shillings in the pound was given on all money spent there. This dividend was my mother's only possible means of saving. In addition no credit charges were made for hire purchase, a very convenient cash saver too. No amount of persuasion would induce mother to buy a press to prevent the racket from warping; never having had one she found the argument hard to believe. I blushed red to the roots when she tried to get away with only buying one ball. I could borrow from my sister couldn't I? But I got them; three in a dark blue string net, one of the few victories over the purse in the ensuing years.

My father took me to Allan's in the town to buy a wooden boxed geometry set. He took little further interest in either the geometry set or my disastrous attempts at maths, but we did go together to buy it.

It became evident that not everyone in my class was overly bright. For the first two school years I was 37th out of 38 pupils. I actually believed that end of term tests were memory tests, not realising that you really had to do revision. Apparently I hadn't noticed that my sister did this when she was forever 'in' and I was forever 'out'.

Snobbery was also evident at Fenham, albeit in a more subtle form. Our music teacher had favourites, invariably children from 'better' backgrounds. She did, however, teach singing well and my love of music started there. We had singing lessons in a beautiful assembly hall. It had a high ceiling, long leaded windows, a shining nun-polished floor and

raised wooden stands at the back. The teacher's choice of pieces was very varied; some my mother had learned at school but many were newer and more challenging. We once learnt *The Pied Piper of Hamlyn* for a public performance. On this occasion, something incredible happened – for that time, anyway – and I imagine more people remember it than the performance. A mother in the front row, clearly a modern mother, breast-fed her baby. Despite the fact that she and it were covered in the essential area by a shawl, it was in its own way revolutionary in a girls' convent school.

Something else that happened in this lovely hall was 'notes'. This was a fortnightly repeated agony for

The Sacred Heart Convent, Fenham Hall Drive, early 1960s. Right, Patricia aged around 14 in 1954.

those unlucky enough to acquire five unsatisfactory marks for work or behaviour. Any class in which a girl had 'lost her note', was obliged to come forward and stand in a half circle in front of the entire staff under the baleful eye of Reverend Mother. The criminal child's name was called out. Severed from the safety of the group, she had to walk up to this frightening figure, who presented her with a small pastel coloured card, 'The Note' on which was printed 'unsatisfactory'. With bowed head she underwent this demeaning process and returned, close to tears, to her place in the ranks. All bowed, and the class returned from whence it came. My sister used to issue black threats of what she would do to me if I 'lost my note'. She found it humiliating to be related to such a renegade. Needless to say she never lost hers. Often my class was called out and sometimes it was my fault. One day someone advised me to show some backbone, and look directly at Reverend Mother when taking the 'note'. That was apparently polite and proper. The consequence was that I was labelled 'brazen' by my class teacher. It made me more awkward and shy than ever.

Patricia Bensdorp Clark

A scholarship to Pendower School

After I passed the scholarship (which my mother was not happy about) I went to Pendower School and always dressed in school uniform. This made me different from the neighbours' children. I had lots of homework to do and was called a swot, but I liked the school and the uniform and was proud to wear it. This was just as well because the headmistress was a strict disciplinarian and made sure we all wore the correct uniform. Until the fourth form we wore navy blue gym tunics, white blouses, gold and blue striped tie and a velour hat in winter. In summer we wore blue and white check dresses, navy blazers and a panama hat. The only thing I didn't like were the navy blue knickers with pockets we wore for gym. When we were older we could wear a navy blue pinafore dresses in winter (which a dressmaker made for me). We always had to wear flat black shoes. I was quite tall and pretty well endowed so could not get a blazer to fit me and my mother had to have one tailor made – very smart it was too. I had to press my own school uniform.

We didn't have a playing field within the school grounds so had to run across the road and up Ferguson Lane to a playing field there. I hated this in the winter months! Another thing I disliked in the winter was the snow. The boys had their playground on the roof and we used to get bombarded with snowballs with no means of fighting back. If we happened to hear the boys shout 'fire', we tried to run for shelter. It didn't always work and we had to stay wet and miserable for the rest of the day.

I used to love Friday afternoons at school because that meant domestic science. The school had a flat near the kitchen where we learned cleaning skills. We learned how to wash and iron, how to wash and look after a baby and do some cooking. Miss Ord, who was in charge of the class, used to inspect us for clean hair tied back, hands and nails spotlessly clean, and that we had the right ingredients if we were cooking. We had to cost out the ingredients too. To this day I enjoy baking.

I remember the headmistress calling me into her office

Mary Dodds

Mary in Paris, in school uniform, 1951.

for a chat regarding uniform. She told me that she needed to see my mother as there was a small sum of money available towards uniforms. Needless to say my mother did not appreciate any kind of charity and did not see the headmistress. My mother worked double shifts to enable me to get all the things I needed (this caused me to become a latchkey kid) but food was always on the kitchen table or in the oven ready to warm up. Even though she disapproved

The rather grim exterior of Pendower School in the mid 1960s.

of my going to that school she worked hard to keep me there.

The boys used the typewriters in our part of the school but they always came down sooner than they should so that they could pull faces at the windows of the classroom. Contact with the boys within a mile of the school was not allowed except at Christmas when we were in the fourth form and they came down for a party and dance. We were allowed to wear anything we wished then. My mother used to knit me a new twinset in lovely colours every year for this 'do'. The teachers always commented on how lovely they were.

I went to Paris with the school in 1951. I was taking French and the teachers thought it would be good to go and practise what we had learned. I also had a pen-pal there whom I met and had dinner with. The journey was by coach and ferry and quite exciting for a 14-year-old.

My music mistress, Miss Pickering, was very enthusiastic and pushed us as far as we could go. She decided that we should 'have a go at Dido and Aeneas'. Auditions were held in the school hall for solo parts, the chorus and non-singing roles. I had the part of Mercury because my voice suited the song, certainly not because I was slim and nimble. At the rehearsals I had to stand on a small tree trunk which wasn't very stable and I was very nervous so the wings on my feet and back shook like mad. They eventually used something more solid for the performances, which were held in Whickham View School. All the costumes were made in our school – the soldiers' shields were made out of silver and gold milk bottle tops stuck to board.

Mary Dodds

Mary Dodds, far right, as Mercury in Pendower School's production of Dido and Aeneas.

Young Ladies

In 1950 I was 16 and in the sixth form at La Sagesse in Jesmond. Each morning I would buy a threepenny return ticket from Dunston into Marlborough Crescent bus station, and then get on a No. 33 trolley bus up to the end of Osborne Road. I was a prefect so wore a striped blazer. Discipline was strict and I can remember one of the boys from the Royal Grammar School requesting a match with our 1st eleven hockey team. 'This is a school for young ladies, not young hooligans', came the thunderous reply from our headmistress, who was a nun. Another time the sixth formers put on a Country and Western Night concert for the school, but we made the unfortunate mistake of wearing trousers (or 'slacks' as they were called then). The entire community of nuns walked out in protest.

Elizabeth Sefton (née Whitfield)

We walked to school until we were around 12 when we rode our bikes. It was a 20-minute walk from Gosforth to Jesmond four times each day. My mother must have been standing with our plates in her hand as it would have been a ten-minute turnaround at lunchtime.

Elspeth Rutter

I attended the Church High Junior School in Jesmond from the mid-1950s. My father drove to work, down Grandstand Road and across Blue House roundabout where he dropped me off to walk to school. But quite often, with my girlish love of horses, I would wait for the coal delivery man who drove his horse and cart down the Great

The North Road and its wide floral verges, mid-1950s.

North Road at that time, pausing to allow his horse to drink at the water trough there.

He would then help me clamber onto the back of the coal cart where, perched on a 'clean' piece of sacking I travelled in style as we trotted, legs dangling, in full school uniform (green hat and satchel obligatory of course) along the Great North Road to Clayton Road junction where I would jump down into the road, wave goodbye and run into school, hoping I hadn't been seen by teachers.

Pru Leach

An RGS schoolboy

After the wartime turmoil my family settled in Hexham, paying £1,600 for a big semi-detached house. I might have left Newcastle for good had I not been awarded a scholarship to the Royal Grammar School which was excellent, as the numbers of famous old boys testify. Most of the staff were highly qualified and interested, apart from four, who ruled with a combination of terror and sarcasm, which contrasts so markedly with today's attitudes. I hesitate to identify them for the sake of their families, but my 86-year-old fellow 'Old Boy' neighbour named them once; indeed still has nightmares about them.

Naked swimming in the unheated pool was another hatred of ours, as was playing rugby. Soccer was a dirty word. The glory days of NUFC passed right over our heads. I do, however, claim to have invented mini-cricket, involving two haversacks for wickets, a soft ball and a prayer book for a bat.

Childhood drifted into adolescence. Teenagers were not invented until those years were far behind us. We had little or no guidance in the prevailing culture of prudery, ignorance and middle-aged snobbery, which ensured I never tasted fish and chips until I was 16, nor was I allowed to laugh at Whitley Bay postcards. And neither was I responsible for hanging Dr Miriam Stoppard's underwear from the school clock tower!

Guy Hall

This Ole House

Rosemary Clooney, 1954

The 1950s Home Front

In 1950 I was a young wife with a two-year-old daughter. After the destruction of the Second World War and all the shortages that followed it, it was almost impossible for young couples to find a home of their own. Like many others, we lived with my husband's parents. I hated it.

The in-laws were very stuffy, snobbish and old fashioned and the house had no modern equipment. I did my washing in a poss tub and ran it through a mangle to remove the excess water. I cleaned the floor with a carpet sweeper. Mother-in-law cooked all the meals so I never had the kitchen to myself unless she was away visiting her married daughter. It certainly wasn't how I thought married life would be.

Fortunately it was a fairly big house, so we were able to have some time to ourselves by colonising the dining room, where we ate our meals and spent the evenings. That didn't mean we had any privacy. My mother-in-law used to snoop round our bedroom while I was out. I always knew because she wasn't subtle enough to cover her traces. Then she would gossip about me to the neighbours and compare my little girl unfavourably to her own daughter's children. I was furious. One day I bought a joke snake – a long spring covered with bright paper. I put it in one of the drawers

GRAINGER BUILDING SOCIETY

ROYAL EXCHANGE BUILDINGS
HOOD STREET
NEWCASTLE UPON TYNE 1

Phone : NEWCASTLE 22617/8

MORTGAGES at 4% INTEREST

GRAINGER BUILDING SOCIETY

EASY STEPS TO HOME OWNERSHIP

so it would jump out and surprise anyone that opened it. Mother-in law never said anything, but she didn't search our room again.

In 1953, after six years of marriage, my husband was given a big promotion. It meant moving to Langley Park in County Durham. I was very nervous about moving to a pit village, but delighted because a house went with the job. We could be a proper family at last.

Agnes Chilton

Tin baths and netties

Many young families had to 'live in' with family members as housing was in short supply. Fortunately we didn't have to rent a room from strangers, as a lot of couples had to, as my mam's aunt had a spare room and we lived there until mid 1950. When my parents were given a property to rent in Walker it meant they had a place of their own to live, but in a way it was a step backwards. The flat was no more than two large rooms with a broom-cupboard sized kitchen. When I say kitchen, I use the term loosely; a sink with a cold tap, an ancient cooker (the model can be viewed in Woodhorn Colliery museum along with various other items that were in everyday use then) and a small bench area. There were four properties to one yard, but one of the downstairs flats was derelict (this was a magnet for mice and rats so most families kept cats and used mouse traps) so only three families used the so-called 'facilities' namely the two outside toilets (netties). My family took it in turn with the other two families to supply the candle, which was used in the winter to stop the toilet from freezing. Nothing was wasted so, after reading the local newspapers, they were cut up and either threaded on to a piece of string or hung onto a nail for use in the nettie. Also in the yard was what was passed as a wash house; this was where the poss tub and mangle were kept. The water had to be heated before you could do any washing. Fine days were great as you could hang the washing in the back lane, but if it was wet, all the washing had to be dried indoors which meant Mam carrying wet washing up the stairs to where we lived and hanging it on rails attached to the ceiling.

Bath night was usually on a Friday and boy was it a chore! The tin bath hung in the yard, so it had to be carried up the stairs and placed in front of the fire (an old black lead range with an oven to the left of the fire and a large mantle piece above). To fill it meant carrying kettles or pans of hot water, which had been boiled on the old gas oven's hobs, back and forward until sufficient water was in the bath. You then took turns to bathe, kids first, then Mam, then Dad last of all.

The whole family shared the one bedroom which had a gas fire, the type with chalky elements that regularly had to be replaced. The fire gave off reasonable heat but the flame burned yellow and blue and made funny little popping noises as it burned. One bedroom looked out onto the No. 19 bus terminus stop and across the road was the Stack Pub. You could look across into it and see the people at the bar, always men as in those days as women rarely went into pubs. There was also a blue police box on the corner next to the Stack which was most fortunate, especially on a Saturday night when there was usually some kind of commotion going on.

The back lane was our playground and social meeting place for mothers. There were always mothers standing at the door to their yard watching us and gossiping with the neighbours. We played simple games like hide and seek, tag, or ring games like The Farmer Wants a Wife. Usually the smallest of your friends was chosen to be the bone as this meant 'the bone' could easily be lifted up!

Oh the joy of eventually moving from Hibernia Street in Walker to Benton. What a novelty to have electric lights and an inside toilet and bath. On cold school mornings you raced downstairs to stand in front of the oven to warm while waiting for the coal fire to be lit. This normally took a while as it needed to be cleaned out first, which meant that all the previous days' coal and ash had to be removed and a new fire laid with paper twisted into strips and maybe a fire lighter before the coal was added. The paper was lit by a match then the blazer (a piece of thin metal with a handle in the centre) was placed over the front of the fire to 'draw' it. After checking to see that the flames were starting, you took the blazer down and hopefully a nice warm fire would be burning in the grate. Often the chimney sweep was required to clean all the soot from the chimney, this was a messy business and covers had to be placed around the fireplace to keep the carpets clean. It was often the children's job to keep running out into the street to watch for the sweep's brush appearing above the chimney. They then had to go back inside and tell the sweep that he could then bring the brushes down again. The water was heated by coal fire or in the summer you were allowed to put the immersion heater on briefly.

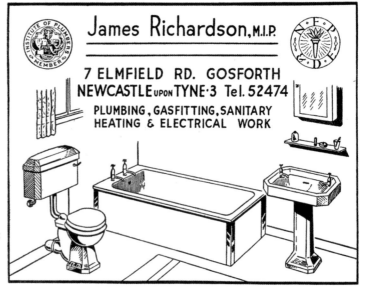

Pat Rogerson

Albert Street, Shieldfield in 1957, earmarked for redevelopment. The tin bath in the yard was the norm for many families in Newcastle, as was the outside nettie.

In 1955 Newcastle City Council Housing Committee looks at the options for new housing.

On 31 May 1955 the Housing Committee stated: 'Not until every family in the city has a decent healthy home with reasonable amenities in decent healthy surroundings will the council relax their efforts'.

The post war slum clearance movement was well underway by the mid 1950s, before Labour regained control of the council in 1958 (on a very narrow vote: they had been out of power since 1951).

My mum did the week's washing on a Monday. This was an all-day job. We had a one-tub washing machine with a wringer on the top and an agitator at the base. The machine was filled with hoses attached to the taps and drained into a bucket and we rinsed in the kitchen sink. The washing was always hung out to dry. The ironing was done on the Tuesday; my mother was always exhausted on Monday and Tuesday nights! We helped out when we weren't at school.

We got a week's grocery order from Wilkinson's on the High Street in Gosforth. This was delivered on a Thursday by a boy on a bike. Because there were no fridges, the meals had to be planned so we ate the most perishable food first. We tended to have the same meals on certain nights. Sunday was the traditional roast, Monday nights we had the roast sliced cold or minced as rissoles, I loved these. Wednesday could be macaroni cheese or tinned tuna. Thursday was grocery order delivery day and we had sausages. Friday was always fish, which we hated, but the cod and turbot were bigger fish than you can get now. We always got the fish from Lilly who stood on Church Avenue once a week. She came up on the train from North Shields to South Gosforth station with her barrow of produce.

Milk was kept cool with a long clay pot over it. This was steeped in cold water and held its temperature. I suppose the butter had a similar clay dish to keep it cool. Cream was from the top of the milk bottle.

We were quite comfortably off, believe it or not. We owned our own house and it had three radiators downstairs, which ran off a coke stove in the kitchen. This was the central heating. In the bedrooms we had small electric bar heaters, but I still remember ice on the insides of the windows on the winter mornings.

Elspeth Rutter

Elspeth's grandparents at their home in Throckley. Doris worked in Marks & Spencer and Josh drove a lorry. The hot water cylinder was in the airing cupboard behind them and the coal fire beside them had a back boiler to heat the water.

My parents lived in a rented terraced house in the poorer end of Heaton with its outside toilet in the back yard, no bathroom and only cold running water. The tin bath hanging in the backyard was still in use I think, but I used to go to one of the council Slipper Baths where for a nominal sum you could take your soap and towel and soak in a hot bath for as long as you liked if there was no queue. What improved the lives of many families was that woman began going out to work and with two wages coming in they were able to improve their standard of living, enjoy greater comforts and look forward with hope to the future.

Joe Pegg

Slum housing

When I worked for the Newcastle School Health Service, I was introduced to the badly run-down parts of the city. The city centre was still post-war shabby, but many of the suburbs were in a dire state. Rye Hill was slowly becoming the area favoured by recent immigrants from the Indian sub-continent. Dark-skinned men in thin, shabby suits shivered on icy, winter pavements. Their wives and children were rarely seen at the weekly clinics for, apart from everything else, there was both a language problem and a considerable amount of resentful racism.

Elswick and Benwell were very run down. Many families lived in dreadful, crowded conditions without bathrooms and with shared outdoor toilets. A fair number had leaky roofs and the crowded flats they occupied were permanently damp. It is easy to blame the landlords for such dreadful conditions, but I should point out that the ownership of many of these properties, built for 19th century workers, had since become an inheritance from a Victorian ancestor now split between numerous descendants who lived elsewhere in the world. The owners' share of the rental was collected weekly but distributed annually by agents. Most probably had several owners, who knew little of the ramshackle nature of the property that was partly theirs.

Many of the children in these areas suffered from weak chests – tuberculosis was still a dreaded scourge in such conditions and skin diseases like scabies, ringworm and impetigo were extremely common.

Within a month of transferring to my new job, Benwell was in the middle of a diphtheria outbreak and children died. The greatest difficulty the medical staff had was in persuading reluctant parents that inoculating their children did protect them.

Maureen Brook

Run down housing in Cambridge Street, Rye Hill, 1959.

Setting up house

With housing shortages and rationing of many goods lasting until 1954, it was not easy for young people to set up home together. Like many couples marrying immediately after the war, my mother and father began married life living first with dad's parents and later with mam's.

Timber shortages meant that the only new furniture being manufactured was 'Utility'. It was rationed. Only newly-weds and people who'd been bombed out of their homes were allowed to buy it. Utility furniture wasn't popular because it was plain. However when Binns managed to get some stock, mam and dad felt lucky to be able to buy two small whitewood chests of drawers. These were sturdy, so regularly repainted and with changes of handles, they served our family well for several decades.

After 1952 when the utility furniture scheme ended, timber became more readily available and choice improved. The following year, dad was promoted within the National Coal Board. With it came the chance to rent a NCB house.

They had saved enough to buy a new bedroom suite. I would have been about 5 years old and remember going with them to Nusenbaum's furniture manufacturers with a showroom on Westgate Road. We spent a long time looking at pattern books, and samples of wood, but most exciting was being shown around the factory. We walked up rickety wooden stairs, along sawdust strewn galleries. Men in white aprons smiled at me as I watched them shape chair legs with chisels. I was fascinated by wood curling from planes to make heaps on the floor.

After the austerity of the utility movement it was unsurprising that mam and dad chose a bleached walnut Queen Anne style suite. The pattern on the wood that made up the wardrobe, dressing table, chest of drawers, bed head and foot boards was skilfully matched. Legs were curvy, the mirror shaped and bevelled, and drawer handles latticed gilt metal.

Tana Durham

All Mod Cons, or 'I'll have one Made at Work'

After the war, father worked at Swan Hunter's shipyard, then one of the biggest employers in the North East. Although father was paid to assist in ship production, he also used any opportunity that arose to apply the firm's services to his creature comforts or ours.

In those days everyone had coal fires and the evidence of that, among other things, were the net curtains that were washed every fortnight – the washing water was totally black. If the weather was bad, the coal-men wore sacks folded over head and shoulders to keep out the rain while supporting the heavy weight of coal.

The fire was one of the sources of domestic conflict if not always conflagration. Father usually set and lit it early in the morning and considered mother inadequate to the task. To let it go out was considered a crime. With the *Daily Herald* and the coal shovel he sealed off the room from the fire and soon had the flames roaring up the chimney or pouring into the room when the paper caught fire, which it did with the regularity of a clock. We didn't own a fireguard and to this day I swear we had an overworked Guardian Angel entreating our safety in the courts above.

At some point logic intervened, and after one of many heated arguments, father announced that he'd 'have a blazer made at work' to replace the paper and shovel. Some time later, when the subject was long forgotten, he staggered in doors sweating and heaving with the blazer in his hands.

'Now you'll see, try that!' he panted. I say hands, not hand, because although a blazer was intended to be light and portable and easily laid aside, he couldn't have lifted it without both hands. It looked more like something designed to protect a Roman legion than encourage Co-op coals to burn. It was made of two plates of ship's steel riveted down the middle, where there was a large handle as thick as a man's thumb. To use the word sturdy was grossly to underestimate its character.

'Ee, Jimmy, don't ye think it's a bit heavy?' mother remarked untactfully.

'Yer never bloody grateful, I'm off to the bar!' and he was, but then again he didn't need an excuse. He was disappointed and irritated by the underwhelming response to his effort. He wouldn't stay to quarrel, he just rushed off; he went every night. Needless to say the blazer was used briefly and symbolically; no one dared to laugh and finally it took years to rust away in a corner of the backyard. Never was there a greater tribute to British Steel.

Workers on their way home from Swan Hunter's, late 1950s. What were they taking home under their coats?

Everything needed coupons in those years. Eventually, everything, including carpets, wore thin and the belief that 'home made is best' wore thinner. Mother made a phenomenal discovery on a trip to the town; skeins of natural-coloured dishcloth cotton. This was soon to be all the rage; dyed and looped through canvas as we all made our own mats. The real trouble started with the dyeing. In her enthusiasm mother had forgotten to tie off the ends of the skeins. When they came out of the dye in rainbow hues, they were in the most incredible tangles and she used to bribe us to spend an hour taking out the knots 'I'll give you threepence!'

'What shall we do for a mat hook?' was the next cry. Father said he'd 'have one made at work'. It's still in my workbox 50 years on, heavy polished steel. Mother developed the muscles of a prize-fighter after spending a whole winter hooking while we unravelled. The mat was greatly admired when finished; a hand drawn design of right and left rising suns and lots of broad stripes, their width depending on the amount of each colour unravelled at the time. 'Come on Patsy, while I make the tea, wind us some green.'

It was large, being made from two sugar sacks sewn down the middle. Its size was its pride and its downfall. Seasons went by and I believe it was Christmas Day, when peace covers the earth; we were all covered with plaster because the ceiling fell down. Father and mother, endeavouring to normalise the situation, picked up the mat at each end to carry away the debris. The debris fell straight through the seam in the middle returning the mat to two sugar bags – coloured. I cannot remember if we laughed or cried

In retrospect it seams quite a miraculous situation that the shipyard made a profit as well as ships. It took a long time for Swan Hunter to finally reach bankruptcy, no doubt aided by the many families 'having one made at work'.

Patricia Bensdorp Clark

Pat Rogerson

A launch at the Swan Hunter yard, possibly the aircraft carrier Albion. All the men are in their Sunday best suits including Pat Rogerson's dad and grandad.

Miners' cottages

I was brought up in a small mining community called Barrington in Northumberland. It was a close knit community where people felt safe enough to leave their doors open during the day. The majority of residents were part of a large extended family network with many relations living in the same street or row.

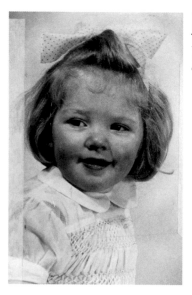

Joan Anderton

There was no hot running water, only one cold tap in the kitchen sink or scullery. Water for bathing or washing clothes was heated up in the boiler in the black fire range, which also had an oven for baking bread, cakes and scones. The huge fireplace was fronted by a strong steel fender and an ample mantelpiece displaying a variety of ornaments and brasses. The brasses had to be polished every week, usually on a Friday. This was a weekly ritual as were a number of household chores; Monday was washing day and Saturday was for baking. I have memories of bathing in front of the fire in a tin bath. Often the same water was used to scrub the washing at the kitchen sink using Sunlight or Fairy washing soap. The clothes were wrung through a large mangle, turning the handle to squeeze the excess water out. Next the clothes were hung on a clothes horse in front of the fire.

Not many women went out to work; the ones that did were either widows or their men were sick and couldn't work. The women's place was in the home and the man was regarded as the head of the household and therefore the bread winner. Because mining was heavy work the housewife had to be there at the end of a shift to provide a substantial meal and hot water for bathing (until the 1950s when showers were installed in the pit changing rooms).

Recreation was going to see a film at the local cinema or visiting the public house a quarter of a mile down the road. I remember two pubs, The Railway Tavern or The Lord Clyde. The Clayton Ballrooms at Bedlington station was where couples met and went dancing.

Joan Anderton

These miners' cottages and their friendly inhabitants, on Dunn Street, Coxlodge, were photographed in the 1950s.

In 1953 the city's 10-year plan for slum clearance stated that 31,518 people in 4,540 houses in 43 streets would be moved from inadequate housing. Noble Street would be first to be followed by Shieldfield, Denton and Scotswood, Elswick, Spital Tongues, Paddy Freemans, the Leazes Park area, Walker and Byker. In April 1953 the first three-storeyed flats on the Corporation's Longbenton Housing Estate opened.

On 15 June 1954 the *Evening Chronicle* noted the compulsory purchase of houses in 15 streets in the Noble Street area of Elswick. In December 1954 *The Journal* quoted Councillor T. Dan Smith of the Housing Committee. He said that 9,728 families were living in 4,538 houses 'not in a fit condition'. More housing was desperately needed, but this needed to tie in with the City Development Plan for more industrial development. In Noble Street itself, five houses contained 21 families comprising 70 people, all needing to be rehoused. Five-storey flats would be built to make a 'pleasant residential area'. It was felt that people would rather be re-housed in the areas where they already lived with their neighbours rather than be moved to outlying estates.

The Queen may be visiting a show house on Tyneside on her journey through the North East, 29 October 1954, in this photograph. Does anyone know where this was?

The work at Noble Street started in early 1956 and other areas of the city were to follow soon, including the Blandford Street area, Shieldfield, Fawdon and North Kenton. Not everyone wanted to move though many were keen to leave the damp and cramped conditions. There were also many grumbles about the housing list. In 1955 plans were also being discussed for a new town to be built outside the city to help eradicate overcrowding and the 'disease' of the slums.

These photos of Noble Street coming down and the
Noble Street flats going up were taken in 1957-8. The
flats would be demolished in 1978, just 20 years after
completion.

Ten Thousand Housewives

In 1954 the firm of Thomas Hedley (part of the Procter & Gamble Group since 1930) opened Sandgate House, a newly converted building on City Road, next door to their Newcastle factory, especially for skin-research, home economics, perfume blending and research, particularly soap product research. 10,000 housewives would visit Sandgate House each year to help the skin research group to ensure 'product mildness' in brands like Daz. Above the skin research department was the perfume lab where products like the shampoo Drene were perfected. It included an odour-free room for testing.

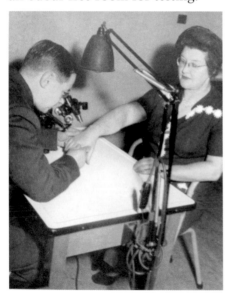

If you want to get ahead, get a hat! Ladies test the kindness to hands of detergents in 1956.

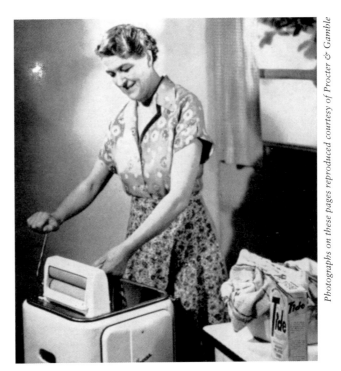

A poss-tub and dolly, often used in the early 1950s, and the latest in washing machines and mangles in 1953.

On the next floor up was the kitchen where three home economists did most of their work. Here you might find one of them at the sink, washing a pair of gloves as part of a wash-wear test; or preparing information about Hedley products in response to a request from a domestic science college. They went out to give lectures and washing demonstrations to women's organisations and to teachers training housewives-to-be.

These evocative photographs are from the Thomas Hedley in-house magazine *Moonbeams*, which featured all the Hedley factories and their staff.

In 1954 Hedley's came up with this memorable billboard advertisement for Daz.

Such a Night

The Drifters, 1954

Out on the town

One of my favourite memories is going to the May-Kway Chinese Restaurant at the top of Northumberland street, practically opposite the Tatler, which showed continual newsreels and cartoons. The May-Kway was one of the first Chinese restaurants in the North East. I was very impressed with the food but too timid to try anything but fried rice for the first year or two. I eventually graduated to trying other dishes but only very cautiously.

I used to meet my father for lunch once a week and we went to the Criterion near Grey's Monument. Another favourite eating place was Tilleys Tea Rooms on Blackett Street – delicious food and wonderful entertainment provided by Jos. Q. Atkinson and his Orchestra. On Saturday mornings my fellow students and I used to meet for coffee at the Terrace Tearooms in Fenwick's.

Elizabeth Sefton (née Whitfield)

In November 1955 Newcastle's first official What's On guide was published. Guides came out monthly through the rest of the decade and into the 1960s, becoming more colourful and more elaborate as the years went by. The first number included selected cinema listings, music, football fixtures, theatre, talks and events and lots of advertising. It was the end of austerity and the beginning of the entertainment age.

The Hit Parade (a new concept) also featured and in November 1955 top of the chart was 'The Man from Laramie' by Jim Young. Bill Haley's 'Rock Around the Clock' only reached number 20.

Newcastle

April 1956

VOL. I   NO. 6

ENTERTAINMENTS

WHATS - ON

The city didn't lure students with the bars, cafés, clubs restaurants of today. The only places to get a fairly early meal were the News Theatre (now the Tyneside Cinema) Café for eggs or beans on toast, or the one exotic foreign restaurant, the Chinese May-Kway, at the top end of Northumberland Street. It closed at nine o'clock.

The Quayside was for shipping offices and other business activities and the River Tyne was full of vessels. I knew of two or three posh and formal restaurants, such as Emerson's, where Waterstone's now is and Tilleys, but our formal dances, our balls, in the Halls of Residence and The Old Assembly Rooms, included meals. We also had marvellous dances at the Oxford Galleries where some terrific 'big bands' such as Joe Loss played the music of Glenn Miller and the great jazz of the period.

By the late 1950s, working and more affluent, I would have coffee in Fenwick's Terrace Tea Room, to the music of Willie Walker's band, or in Bainbridge's where mannequins would display the latest fashions and the tea room overlooked the Bigg Market.

Maureen Callcott

In a courtyard off the Groat Market was the Chinese restaurant favoured by Hedley's staff and Town Hall workers where for 1s 6d or a luncheon voucher you could have a two-course meal. The choice of pudding was always either ice cream or a banana in batter.

We could go dancing at the Oxford Galleries with its marvellous sprung floor and great dance bands. Or we could choose the posher Old Assembly Rooms, also extremely popular.

The clubs that were just beginning to open up were beyond the income of most youngsters, and the laws concerning alcohol consumption were taken very seriously, so we did not drink, nor did we expect to be offered alcohol until we were 18. I suspect that some of the boys got away with it, but it just did not occur to most girls to attempt to thwart the laws.

Maureen Brook

Westgate Road Snack Bar, 1958.

For a formal occasion in the evening, the restaurant of choice was always Tilleys, then in Blackett Street. I can remember asking the conductor of the orchestra one evening if they would play *Once I had a Secret Love*, though who the secret love was I have no idea. More racy dining-out was at the Criterion or the Pineapple Grill and sometimes one was taken for a very sophisticated cocktail to the bar at the Turk's Head Hotel, opposite the Theatre Royal.

We went daringly to a Chinese restaurant in Bath Lane, off Westgate Road, where we were served, inscrutably, Chop Suey and Sweet and Sour Pork at plain wooden tables in an ill-lit undecorated room; we thought it romantic and mysterious.

Jane Jantet

Tilleys, Blackett Street, for 'discerning people', with doorman to keep out the rif-raf, around 1956.

Fine dining at the restaurant at the Odeon Cinema. This photograph was taken on 12 February 1955.

EATING OUT

A *pleasure*
to serve you

FOR GOOD FOOD —
WELL AND QUICKLY
SERVED

CARRICK'S
Cafes and Snackbars
THERE'S ONE CLOSE BY !

Top, the Grainger Street branch of Carrick's around
1957. Right the Market Street branch, beneath the
Labour Party office, around 1950.

Grammar School drinkers

From some points of view – male that is, and doubtless especially young male – Newcastle in the 1950s was a world of pubs. From another, female perspective of course it was nothing of the kind: the pubs were invisible among the much brighter, more attractive world of Bainbridge's, Binns and Fenwick's, where, for middle-aged ladies, the delights of shopping and coffee with 'the girls' (diaries out, and 'Where shall we three meet again?') far outshone the dull masculine quest for a pint; a quest to be satisfied in the spaces between the brilliant shop windows of the department stores, in the almost invisible narrow frontages of another, lower species of commercial premise. Where the boys and girls met on equal, undifferentiated terms, of course, was in the library of the Lit and Phil, since none of the boys (or the girls either, I suppose) would deny any of their intellectual pretensions just because they went to the pub as well. Beer and the life of the mind were if not identical at least parallel, mutually supporting pillars of life in the metropolis of the North.

An underage drinker in school uniform in 1958.

What we drank horrifies me now. Newcastle Brown Ale, that sweet, strong liquid, had prestige. Perhaps points were scored in proportion to the pain of drinking it. The alternative was the various, less prestigious products of the Vaux Breweries, which, if easier to get down, were duller in their effects. The faint-hearted were punished with Merrydown Cider, the pleasant taste of which hid much more lethal consequences than the beer. We thought it rather girly, but secretly liked it better, though not, of course, its inevitable consequences.

As to pubs, we started with the Brandling Arms, or the Collingwood, which were conveniently close to school. The discipline in both school and pub was lax enough to allow us a pleasant lunchtime pint, albeit we were (I would have thought obviously, and in the case of some of us blatantly) under 18. These were agreeable pubs where our fathers might have drunk on a Saturday lunchtime (we were always there on a weekday, so avoided the ghastly experience of meeting an ancestor at the bar); the closest thing, perhaps, to a Home Counties Golf Club waterhole. The lunchtime pint did none of us any harm; in fact it probably prepared us for the civilized drinking of our married, suburban futures, a prospect that we would certainly not have been prepared to admit, had it occurred to us.

Evenings were another matter. Downtown pubs offered a variety of delights. On the Quayside was the Anchor, the clients of which were a mixture of businessmen and intellectuals, the latter category staying until closing time. When we went there we were impressed by the local Sartres and the occasional Simone de Beauvoir, whose discourse we did not really understand. In retrospect I suppose it was the resort of the university, but of this we were unaware. Like the Brandling, it was educational. At the other end of the Quay was the Baltic, a run-down place that we liked especially, where the elderly barmaid might be asked by a rather forward customer, 'Yer liked a bit of how's yer father, didn't yer hinny?' 'Aye…'

But best of all was the Royal Court. The Royal Court was in the Bigg Market, down a flight of stairs, always a hopeful outward sign of seedy decadence. The décor was a faded sub-Mark-Gertler mural of circus horses and gaudy carriages. The bar was a long loop, I think, without much depth, so most people crowded up to the bar, where there was usually room; the effect was like being on stage. It was supposed to be mildly dangerous, though I never saw any evidence of it; the clients in fact were remarkably welcoming to green intruders on a pub crawl. Perhaps they were more theatrical than dangerous, but that was the impression it amused them to give.

Of course this is only one survivor's impression of Newcastle's innumerable pubs: other people went to the Eldon Grill, the Albert, the Scotswood Road pubs; there were so many pubs on the Scotswood Road that wags would play a game, a pint in every pub, but if you had to pee you had to go back a pub – nobody ever got to the end. But we didn't compete in that game. We were grateful for the pubs we did visit, and for the lax regime which allowed us, quite illegally, though nobody seemed to mind, to get used to the Demon Drink.

Jeremy Catto

The Bigg Market, late 1950s. The coffee drinkers in Bainbridge's could look down on the stalls from the first floor café. They could also just about see the entrance to the Royal Court, should they have wished to. Note the police box beside the public toilets.

… Another place I loved was Pumphrey's Coffee House in the Cloth Market. You could smell the inviting aroma of roasting coffee as you walked down the street to Pumphrey's. They sold coffee and tea and upstairs was a beautiful little café, which was panelled in polished wood with an alcove for each table. The tables had polished copper tops, with a fixed bench seat each side, and above the bench was a corded net rack on cast iron brackets, where you could put your briefcase while you were drinking the most delicious coffee. Tony Finn

At the hop

We went to dances, to dance the Quickstep (slow, slow, quick quick, slow) and the Foxtrot. We taught ourselves to do the Tango and the Samba.

Jane Jantet

There were lots of dance halls. In the city centre there was the Old Assembly Rooms, which was popular for private dances and functions and the Oxford Galleries, which was the lively one. It had a really good band and a female singer.

Out of town there was the Heaton Ballroom and the Wallsend Memorial Hall in the east end. Ringtons Tea also hosted a dance. In the west end we could choose from Scotswood Dance Hall, The Milvain Ballroom and the Brighton. Several churches held dances including St Bede's, St Lawrence, Benwell Parish Church and St Gabriel's. Some of the Co-op stores, including Walbottle, held dances above the shops. If you were willing to travel a bit further, there were several dances at the coast.

I particularly liked the Brighton Ballroom on Westgate Road. It was a bit more sedate – not much Rock'n'Roll but plenty of waltzes, Foxtrots, and Quicksteps. There was also the Bradford Barn – always popular with the chaps with two left feet who couldn't dance well. After a few dance steps you changed partners so it was a great opportunity for boys who were too shy or clumsy to ask a girl to dance.

If you really wanted to let your hair down, the Heaton Ballroom, with Les Feeney and his band, was the place for the Big Boppers (serious Rock'n'Rollers). When the band played *Rock Around the Clock* or *St Louis Blues*, the dance floor rocked never mind the dancers. I was always a spectator and never a rocker.

Mabs Taylor

Dancing opportunities in a 1958 What's On guide.

DANCING

2132 4 **OXFORD GALLERIES.**
Every evening. Afternoons on Mons.
Weds. and Sats. at 3 p.m.

HEATON BALLROOM.
Mons. Weds. Fris. and Sats.

BRIGHTON BALLROOM.
Old Time Tues. and Sats. at 7 p.m.
Modern Thurs. and Fris. at 8 p.m.

OLD ASSEMBLY ROOMS.
Every Sat. at 7.30 p.m.

MAJESTIC BALLROOM.
Every evening at 7.30 p.m. Tea
Dances — Weds. and Sats. at 3 p.m.
10th June "Queen of the Sun" Ball

Above, the Heaton Ballroom, Heaton Road, in 1961.

Right, the Milvain in 1960, just after a fire had destroyed the upper floor.

I was a teenager in the 1950s, but we were not wild! The town was our playground. We used to go to see bands on a Sunday night at the Odeon, but there were no cinemas open. There was Mark Toney, or you could walk to the Globe in Gosforth (which could open, not being in Newcastle). And there was the News Theatre Coffee Rooms. That was a wonderful place. Mr Williams was the manager. It was for men only except on a Saturday when women were allowed in.

For dances we used to go mainly to the Oxford (which cost 1s 6d) and to a hall at Westerhope called The Institute, or Tute. We'd get the bus up past Cowgate but we used to walk all the way back and get chips on the way home. I dated a lad when I was about 17. He played in a band at the Tute. He's an accountant now.

I went to the West End Boys club on Severus Rd when they opened a section for girls. I'd be 15 or 16. The man that ran the club taught the girls to dance. The dances were great, like the Gay Gordons or the Quick Step. They lads that went were men's men but they'd get up and dance.

The first place I ever jived was at the Banqueting Hall in Jesmond. My mam used to work for Newcastle Breweries and did outside catering there.

Mary McArdle

The Oxford, 1949.

The George Hornsby Band performs at the Milvain dance hall, West Road, 1951.

Left, an advert dated 1956.

Youth Clubs

In 1952 I joined the choir in St Margaret's Church on Armstrong Road and consequently became a member of the youth club, which was on Norland Road. It was here that I became a table tennis player, did some handicrafts and enjoyed dancing. I was put in charge of a group of young girls who did country dancing on the Town Moor. At about the same time a neighbour, who was a great supporter of a boy's football team, took me to watch one of the matches in Scotswood and from then on I supported them, taking them oranges for half time each week.

I was then introduced to Murray House Community Centre, which was near the Big Lamp on Westgate Road. The warden, Mr Gresham, saw that I was interested in 'lending a hand' so he encouraged and supported me to get more involved in youth work (which I did in later life). I played table tennis and travelled to other youth clubs with a team to compete in the table tennis league. A clog/tap dancer came to the centre to teach the younger members how to dance. I helped him with the really young children and at the end of the year he gave me a certificate.

Another exciting time was the visit of Lord and Lady Mountbatten to the Community Centre (the Centre had ties with the Admiralty) and I shook hands with them both.

One night in 1955 we were holding a dance at the Youth Club and suddenly all went quiet as one of the boys entered the hall wearing a Teddy Boy suit. It was blue and he also had blue suede shoes, He looked strange to us as his hair was done in a DA and it was the first time we had seen a Teddy Boy!

I loved singing and when the Youth Club decided to put on a 'show' I sang solo and was extremely nervous even though I had done lots of singing with the school choir and went to the City Hall every year for the Schools' Choir Competition.

Mary Dodds

Pat Fairless

96

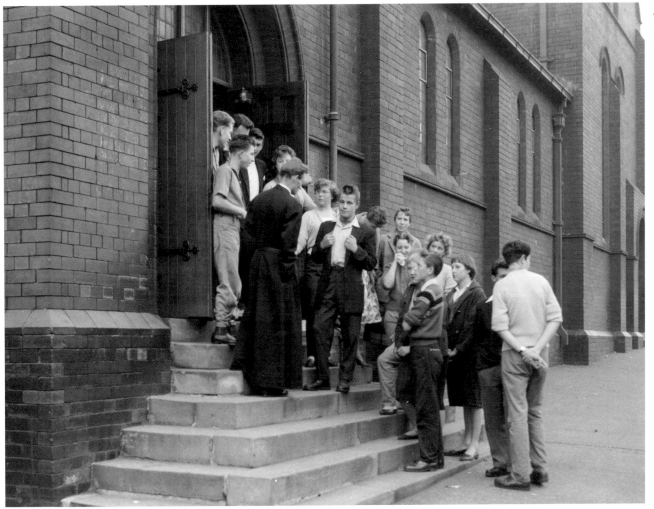

The youth club at St Lawrence's Church, St Peters, 1958. Church youth clubs were great places for young people to get together in the 1950s. They weren't necessarily all that religious.

Left the St Lawrence's youth club skiffle band, 1958.

Going to the pictures

We often went to the Theatre Royal to see plays and musicals and there was a very good choice of cinemas, from the cosy little Grainger on Grainger Street to the bigger ones like the Queen's, off Northumberland Street, and the Odeon on Pilgrim street. I saw *The African Queen*, *Singing in the Rain* and *Doctor in the House*.

Elizabeth Sefton (née Whitfield)

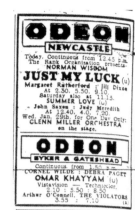

The Grainger Cinema in 1956, and, right, just one column of the cinema listings from the Evening Chronicle January 1958. The Grainger would close in 1960.

Crowds in the Queen's Cinema in 1958. Suburban cinemas were beginning to close during the 1950s with the advent of television, but in the city centre they flourished, showing blockbusters.

We went to the cinema endlessly – the West Jesmond, the Odeon, the Stoll and knew the names of all the stars, falling hopelessly in love with them all.

Jane Jantet

For entertainment there were the cinemas in the Haymarket, Northumberland Street and three on Westgate Road, including the old Stoll which showed naughty films such as *Nudes in the Snow*.

Maureen Brook

In the 1950s Newcastle had not only a staggering number of cinemas but also a number of variety theatres. After the working day was through the town came to life again with the theatre and cinema crowds. The Empire and The Palace, with their brightly lit facades, attracted the crowds out for a night's enjoyment where they saw various variety acts and a world class singer or band or other attraction 'topping the bill'. Cinemas ranged from the opulent, Odeon or Essoldo to the plush Queen's and Haymarket, the older Stoll and Pavilion to the more intimate and discerning Grainger or Tatler or News Theatre.

We were spoilt for choice when it came to films. Most cinemas had continuous performances which, in theory at least, meant for the price of admission you could go into the cinema in the morning sit through performance after performance and come out after the last show finished late evening. At the end of the last performance it was common practice to play the National Anthem with a picture of the King or Queen against a fluttering Union Jack on the screen and for everyone to stand to attention. Collective pride, respect and discipline were still around in the 1950s.

Joe Pegg

Byker cinemas. Top, the Regal advertises in 1955, and right, the Brinkburn in 1957, looking a little sorry for itself. The children's matinee seems to be top of the bill. In 1960 it closed.

REGAL THEATRE
BYKER, NEWCASTLE.

Sunday, November 6th.
OLSON and JOHLSEN in " HELLZAPOPPIN " (U)
GEORGE RAFT in " ESCAPE ROUTE " (U)

Nov. 7th for 6 days.
Cinemascope with Sterophonic Sound.
JANET LEIGH and JACK LEMMON in " MY SISTER EILEEN (U)
JACK KELLY in " THE NIGHT HOLDS TERROR " (A)

Sunday, Nov. 13th.
BOB HOPE and BING CROSBY in " ROAD TO ZANZIBAR " (U)
JEAN KENT and JOHN BENTLEY in " THE LOST HOURS " (U)

Nov. 14th for 6 days.
BERT LANCASTER in " THE KENTUCKIAN " (U)
BILL ELLIOT in " DIAL RED ' O ' " (A)

Sunday, Nov. 20th.
JOHN LOADER in " MASKED AVENGER " (A)
STANLEY HOLLOWAY in " ONE WILD OAT " (A)

Nov. 21st for 6 days.
DEAN MARTIN and JERRY LEWIS in " YOU'RE NEVER TOO YOUNG " (U)
ALISTAIR SIM and KATHLEEN HARRISON in " SCROOGE "

Sunday, 27th Nov.
BOB HOPE in " MY FAVOURITE BLONDE " (U)
SONIA DRESDEL in " THE THIRD VISITOR " (A)

Martin Nellist, who was at Newcastle University in the 1950s, took this splendid shot of the Haymarket Cinema with hearthrob Frankie Vaughan, looking moody, top of the bill in October 1957 as the Rag Parade majorettes marched along Percy Street.

The Sunday Entertainments Act of 1932 allowed cinemas to open on Sundays but Newcastle electors didn't vote for Sunday opening until 1952, and licences were not issued until 1953. Even then, most cinemas could only get cheaper or older films because of the problems of restricted opening hours and Sunday transport. Only the Haymarket was canny enough to start its weekly programme on a Sunday, so ensuring a full house. Other city centre cinemas followed suit, and the Odeon, Essoldo and Westgate abandoned Sunday concerts in favour of movies. Fears of 'hooliganism' proved unfounded.

The Odeon, 1951. Night Without Stars starring David Farrar and Nadia Gray was showing.

Starlet Dawn Addams, Jack Warner and commentator Leslie Mitchell, outside the Odeon, 8 November 1951.

On 8 November 1951, Newcastle's film fans enjoyed a treat when 15 stars of screen arrived at the Central Station to attend a replica Royal Film Performance of 'Where No Vultures Fly' at the Odeon. The train was 13 minutes late, arriving soon after 3.15pm, with its fireman sporting a trilby hat! According to news reports, the crowd was youthful with 'girls in office and shop overalls, fur coats and summer dresses, and the welcoming party included dozens of the daughters of porters, railway clerks, railway canteen assistants and other teen-agers with some connection with the railway.' More than 2,000 people cheered the arrival of British and American stars including Googie Withers, Jane Russell, Richard Todd, Jack Hawkins, Veronica Hurst and Fred MacMurray, as well as the stars of the film, Dinah Sheridan and Anthony Steel.

Left to right, Leslie Mitchell, Jane Hylton, Harry Watt (?), Veronica Hurst, Anthony Steel, Dawn Addams.

After retiring to the Station Hotel, six Rolls Royces took the stars to the Odeon for a 7pm reception. Pilgrim Street was packed with people waiting for a glimpse of their favourite stars. A platform was set up outside the Odeon and film commentator Leslie Mitchell introduced the galaxy of stars. It was 'a memorable night for bobby-soxers'. Dinah Sheridan charmed the crowds on her arrival by stating 'I have been here so many times that it is almost like another home for me. I love it!'

The stars' clothes were described in loving detail. Jane Hylton wore a ballet-length dress in pleated transparent silk, which fell in tiers over yellow taffeta with yellow sash. Googie Withers wore sea-green shantung.

Over 2,500 people were seated in the cinema for the performance of the command film.

Left to right Jane Hylton, Veronica Hurst, Dan Duryea, Van Johnson, Anthony Steel, John McCallum, Dawn Addams, Googie Withers, Fred MacMurray, Jack Warner (behind Peter Reynolds).

There was glamour for local girls too. Twenty-four Newcastle girls were chosen from the staff at John Moses and Fenwick on the basis of 'looks, personality, intelligence and deportment', to sell programmes. The Fenwick's girls wore dresses in golden yellow and twilight grey, half ballet, half party frock, with satin and net. They carried Dorothy bags, wore mauve gloves and shoes, and heavy gold jewellery. Their hair was sprayed with gold.

In contrast to the lavishness on display on 8 November, the Journal headlines read: 'ECONOMY CUTS WILL HIT FOOD' and 'FINANCIAL CRISIS: FOOD IMPORTS TO BE CUT!'

The gorgeousness of the Odeon in the 1950s (seen here in 1957), was a welcome antidote to the rather grey reality of many people's daily grind.

ODEON CINEMA

Sun., Nov. 6. " BEYOND THE BLUE HORIZON "

Mon., 7. " THE TROUBLE SHOOTER "
ROBT. MITCHUM — JAN STIRLING
" STOLEN TIME "

Sun., 13. " UNTAMED "

Mon., 14.
JOE MACBETH — PAUL DOUGLAS — RUTH ROMAN
" A DUEL ON THE MISSISSIPPI "

Sun., Nov. 20. " SMUGGLER'S ISLAND "

Mon., 21. " RAWHIDE YEARS "
TONY CURTIS — COLLEEN MILLER
" TIMESLIP "

Sun., Nov. 27. " APACHE TRAIL "

GAUMONT CINEMA

Sun., Nov. 6. " RAIDERS OF THE SEVEN SEAS "
" MAGAMBO "

Mon., 7. " LUCY GALLANT "
Technicolor.
JANE WYMAN — CHARLTON HESTON
" THE SILVER STAR "

Sun., Nov. 13. " SOMEWHERE IN THE NIGHT "

Mon., 14. SUMMER MADNESS "
KATHRYN HEPBURN — ROFFANO BRAZZI
Technicolor
" MURDER IS MY BEAT "

Sun., 20. " APPOINTMENT WITH VENUS "
Mon. 21st—See Press Announcements.

Sun. 27th—" SUDDEN FEAR "

Mon. 28th—" SECOND GREATEST SEX " Technicolor C/scope.
Jeanne Crain — George Neder — Mamie Van Doren
" THE VANISHING AMERICAN "

City centre cinemas advertise in November 1955.

PAVILION   NEWCASTLE

Sunday,   RICHARD BASEHART   GARY MERRILL
November 6th   " DECISION BEFORE DAWN " (A)
Nov. 7th   JANE WYMAN   ROCK HUDSON
for 6 days. " ALL THAT HEAVEN ALLOWS " (U) Technicolor.
ALEC GUINNESS " THE MAN IN THE WHITE SUIT " (U)

Sunday, Nov. 13th.
BING CROSBY, CHARLES BICKFORD " RIDING HIGH " (U)
" CHARLIE THE PERFECT LADY " (U) CHARLIE CHAPLIN
Nov. 14th   JANET LEIGH,   JACK LEMMON, BETTY GARRETT
for 6 days. " MY SISTER EILEEN " (U) Cinemascope and Technicolor.
JACK KELLY   VINCE EDWARDS
" THE NIGHT HOLDS TERROR " (A)

Sunday, Nov. 20th.
GARY COOPER, ROBERT PRESTON, RAY MILLAND and
SUSAN HAYWARD in " BEAU GESTE " (A)
Nov. 21st for 6 days.
BURT LANCASTER, DIANNE FOSTER, DIANA LYNN
" THE KENTUCKIAN " (U) Cinemascope and Technicolor.
BILL ELLIOTT, KEITH LARSEN " DIAL RED O " (A)

Sunday,   BOB HOPE   PAULETTE GODDARD
Nov. 27th   " THE CAT AND THE CANARY " (A)
DEREK BOND " QUIET WOMAN " (U)
Nov. 28th for 6 days.
DEAN MARTIN   JERRY LEWIS
" YOU'RE NEVER TOO YOUNG " (U) VistaVision & Technicolor.
ALISTAIR SIM as Charles Dicken's SCROOGE " (U)

A.B.C. HAYMARKET

6th November—(7 days)
JOHN WAYNE - LANA TURNER - DAVID FARRAR
" THE SEA CHASE " (U)
Cinemascope — Warnercolor
Wild Bill Elliott, Virginia Grey " THE FORTY MINERS " (U)

13th November. (7 days)
ALASTAIR SIM   BILL TRAVERS
" G E O R D I E " (U)
Technicolor
John Bentley - Hy Hazell " STOLEN ASSIGNMENT " (U)

27th November. (7 days)
DORIS DAY   JAMES CAGNEY
CAMERON MITCHELL
" LOVE ME OR LEAVE ME " (A)
Cinemascope — Eastman Color

Edgar Lustgarten — " THE STATELESS MAN " (U)

Cinemas were everywhere and it wasn't unusual to have to queue for a popular film I remember Mam and I queuing outside the Scala on Chillingham Road for almost half an hour to see *Rose Marie*. There were usually two films shown in those days, the B film, then the Pathe News, trailers for future films, then the main feature A film followed by the National Anthem when everyone stood.

Pat Rogerson

Entertainment was available on the [Shields] 'road' as well, with a number of picture houses to choose from and all within a half mile – Apollo, Black's Regal, Brinkburn and Imperial.

Joe Rogerson

I went to the cinema a lot, especially at art school. I went to a local cinema as a kid. I was hooked early. I saw lots of films, as there would be double bills and they'd change halfway through the week. It was the Classic in Low Fell. We called it The Ranch because there were so many westerns.

Once I got to art school I was in a cinema two or three times a week as there was such a choice. ABC Haymarket, Odeon, Pavilion, Essoldo, the Stoll for art movies, and those wonderful science fiction movies with giant ants and spiders and the incredible shrinking man. All paranoid cold war and nuclear bomb allegories! *High Noon* was supposed to be an allegory for the McCarthy witch hunts. The director was on the blacklist.

At the Stoll you could see art house movies (because they could get them cheap), French, Swedish … people thought they'd see some sexy stuff. I saw *Breathless* – Jean Paul Belmondo and Jean Seberg, *RIFIFI* – the first bank heist caper movie, *The Wages Of Fear*, *Les Diabolique*s – all groundbreakers from French cinema

The News Theatre on Pilgrim Street was all newsreels and cartoons and similar to The Tatler, which was further up Northumberland Street. The Tatler Tearoom upstairs served lunch and high tea. When mam took me shopping we always went there. There was a man playing background music on a grand piano and waitresses in black with white lace caps and pinnies.

John Steel

Above, the Majestic, Benwell, around 1955. It would reach the end of its life in 1961. Many suburban cinemas put on Saturday shows for children as they staved off decline.

I went to Jesmond Picture House, the Jezzy, for the Saturday afternoon show. It was easy to walk to via Johnson's corner shop for chews and my favourite, a tiny plastic cup containing a delectable fondant like a soft dolly mixture. I had ninepence for the pictures and sometimes had money for a red ice lolly too (my teeth were not good, unsurprisingly, and I was terrified of the dentist with his drill). The cinema was full of kids like me. Bugs Bunny or Tom and Jerry first, followed by a cowboy, or Flash Gordon, or Zorro (everyone cheered). The usherette ('the wifey') with her searchlight torch would yank out anyone who caused too much trouble.

Anna Flowers

The Clouded Yellow: filmed in Newcastle

Taking its title from the name of a rare butterfly, *The Clouded Yellow* (released in the UK in late 1950) is a spy thriller following a double-crossed MI6 agent called Somers (played by Trevor Howard) and a young girl, Sophie (Jean Simmons), as they flee north from the authorities in London. With our local architecture still cloaked in its industrial-era grime, the black and white photography of this movie gives its Tyneside scenes a distinctly noir and even gothic feel.

The couple both arrive at and depart from Newcastle by water, emphasising the persisting importance of the River Tyne in the city's commercial life during the early Fifties. As they disembark from a London steam packet onto a bustling quayside, the Tyne Bridge looms over a port busy with merchant vessels and tugs. Their later escape, via rowing boat from the Swing Bridge, is made all the more dramatic as they narrowly evade the searchlight of the River Police launch.

The police are constantly in pursuit and we see shots of detectives on the lookout in the Central Railway Station, then at the old Haymarket Bus Station, with the soot-blackened tower of St Thomas's Church in the distance. The elusive duo manage to board a corporation No. 31B trolleybus on St Nicholas Street (with the Castle Keep in the background) and Somers asks the conductor for 'Two to Jesmond, please.' (Not that the 31B really went to Jesmond.) Inside the bus, an advertisement for Essoldo Cinemas can clearly be seen above his head, whilst through the window they are seen to be passing the Victoria and

Screen shot by Christopher Goulding

The stars round the corner of St Nicholas Street.

Comet pub in Neville Street. The outside of the bus carries a poster for another since-defunct business, Vaux Breweries. Alighting on the Great North Road, with the tower of the Fleming Hospital just visible in the background, they hasten to a rendezvous at a 'safe' house in Burdon Terrace, behind which we see the distinctive tower of Jesmond United Reformed Church.

A further clandestine meeting ensues at a shop situated in an unidentifiable side street in the city centre. Here we meet Kyra, daughter of the East European

Trevor Howard on board the 31B trolleybus.

proprietor and the only character in the film who is supposedly a Geordie, though her accent (general-purpose 'drama school northern') has more to do with the Yorkshire-Lancashire border than with Tyneside. Arrangements are made for the next stage of Somers and Sophie's escape, which is to take place that night at 'the old steps, near the Surtees House.' Here, they make their way to the waiting rowing boat from the foot of the Dickensian-looking and fog-bound Castle Stairs.

Notwithstanding the inevitable solecisms that may be spotted in this film by veterans of the period ('surely the 31B never went up Neville Street...?'), one irritation that's impossible to ignore is the acknowledgement in the film's end credits to the city authorities of somewhere they call 'Newcastle-on-Tyne' [sic]. The shortening of 'upon' and those superfluous hyphens are just unforgivable.

Christopher Goulding

Magic Moments: City Hall classics

For a brief period from the late 1940s until the mid 1950s Newcastle enjoyed an unprecedented period of world-class musical culture in the form of concerts and recitals at the City Hall. The world's leading symphony orchestras, legendary conductors, famous instrumentalists and world class singers began appearing there, all at an affordable price. I took it all for granted at the time but there is no doubt it was a Golden Age in the City Hall's history and unprecedented in a town that had never shown any interest in a higher musical culture. It seems to have been the brainchild of a number of Impresarios who decided that it was what the public needed after being starved of culture during the war years and so they toured world class artists around the country and Newcastle was on the circuit. There were one or two would-be concert promoters who also contributed to the idea, but diminishing returns brought them financial ruin.

At the same time as the concerts at the City Hall there was Italian Opera at the Theatre Royal given by an international company of leading opera singers mostly from Italian Opera Houses. To complement this there were showings at the Grainger Cinema of a series of Italian Opera films, some of the stars of which turned up in concert at the City Hall. The occasional classical artist that had featured in some Hollywood musical film of the period also appeared at the City Hall, which added to the excitement. It was a classical music bonanza not to be repeated.

Joe Pegg

Programmes loaned by Joe Pegg

Don't Let the Stars Get in your Eyes

My memories of attending matinee performances of light operettas at the Theatre Royal are very special. I saw *The Student Prince*, *The Merry Widow*, *Dancing Years on Ice*, and *The King and I*, and these excursions made me feel very grown up. I was expected to be on my best behaviour. Fortunately the singing, dancing, costumes and scenery transported me spellbound to other times and foreign lands so I had no difficulty sitting still and absorbing every colourful detail.

The whole experience was far removed from reality. In daylight we would pass beneath the imposing pillars and climb the stone steps to the plush red velvet and polished brass interior. Our favourite seats were at the front of the Dress Circle. While waiting for the performance to begin I would admire the ornate interior, read the safety curtain, and enjoy listening to the orchestra. Then the lights would dim, the curtain would rise and we would enter a warm and sunny world full of colour and music.

Tana Durham

PROGRAMME

THEATRE ROYAL
NEWCASTLE-ON-TYNE

MESSRS. HOWARD AND WYNDHAM LTD.
Managing Director: Stewart Cruikshank

PLEASE REFUSE PROGRAMME IF SEAL IS BROKEN
6d

My colleagues at the College of Commerce, both clerical and academic, were extremely kind to this ingénue and my lady colleagues took on the task of widening my cultural horizons by introducing me to the Theatre Royal where I saw ballet with Robert Helpmann and Margot Fonteyn and acting stars such as Charles Laughton, Dilys Laye, Albert Finney and the superb, locally raised star, Dame Flora Robson.

There was also the Empire on Westgate Road you could see popular television comedians, such as Ken Dodd or Tony Hancock, in the flesh.

Maureen Brook

We bought books at Mawson Swan & Morgan, and I went alone to the Theatre Royal, up in the Gods, to see *The Cocktail Party*, which gave me a lasting love of T.S. Eliot's work. The Theatre Royal was very grand, all dark red velvet; I remember pantomimes sitting in the front row of the circle, laughing helplessly at the antics of some comic who called everyone 'daft as a brush' as he capered about on the stage.

Jane Jantet

I remember going to the Empire Theatre in Newgate Street with Mam and Dad to see my first show. I believe the star was singer David Whitfield, and both he and the supporting cast were wonderful. I was very sad when the Empire closed and was demolished; it was the end of a splendid auditorium.

Tom Smith

The magic of the Palace Theatre, Percy Street in the early 1950s.

114

Vincent at the Laing

It was Newcastle's art exhibition of the decade. In fact, some visitors to the Laing Art Gallery during its six-week run there in early 1956 claimed that it was the most spectacular since its opening half a century earlier.

For me it was a dream come true. Vincent Van Gogh had been my hero since I first became interested in art, and the thought that more than 130 of his drawings and paintings, spanning his all too brief career of only ten years, would be on show in Newcastle for all those weeks just seemed incredible. But fate was to deliver an unexpected turn of events to make the exhibition even more special for me as I was to be one of the temporary attendants, recruited to protect it from damage or theft.

The sight that greeted us as the doors opened on Higham Place on February 11th was overwhelming. Hundreds had queued for hours to feast their eyes on what, over the coming weeks, were to become the most discussed – and sometimes criticised – works ever to go on show at the Laing. And it wasn't long before I found myself not only one of their guardians, but unofficial guide to the exhibition.

I was overheard one day holding forth on the virtues – as I saw them – of a particular painting that had come in for a mixed reception, and from then on visitors began to ask for me to take them around the show. One such request had an amusing, if somewhat embarrassing consequence, however.

A party of Newcastle University fine art students asked if I would take them around the exhibition towards its close on March 24th. I noticed as we progressed around the galleries that they became increasingly giggly, but had no suspicion of what was to happen when we came to the last, or what I thought was the last, painting on display. Suddenly the giggling stopped and I found myself being scrutinised with eager anticipation. 'This painting,' I began, then stopped in my tracks, for I had never seen it before! The party exploded into laughter, for it was a painting they had knocked up at the university to look like a Van Gogh, and fixed to the wall to throw me.

Marshall Hall

The Goggle Box

Before May 1953, the only way to receive television in the North East was by having an extremely large aerial with vertical polarisation on top of the house. This large aerial was required because the nearest transmitter was at Holme Moss, near Manchester which was really meant to serve only the Manchester area. On good days, a signal could be received as far north as here, but the pictures were very grainy and liable to regular fading.

However, 1953 saw the Coronation of HM Queen Elizabeth II, and in order that people in this area could watch the great event live, the BBC brought forward its plans for opening the Pontop Pike transmitter near Anfield Plain. Test transmissions from Pontop Pike began on a temporary low power transmitter on Monday 20th April 1953, the regular full power transmitter coming into service later in the year. The first programmes were transmitted on Friday 1 May, and you may find the local newspaper's review of the first evening's programmes of interest:

An advert from 1958. Renting was cheaper.

The first evening offered first class entertainment. The visit to the Severn Wildfowl Trust Sanctuary must have been delightful to nature lovers and was excellently produced, the close shots of the birds being particularly fine. The Boys Brigade display from the Royal Albert Hall, London, was another good outside broadcast, and had an efficiency worthy of the Horse Guards Parade. The programme In The News is usually well worthy of attention; last night's discussion of the M.I.G. reward offer was given many interesting angles. Kaleidoscope is a show for the family. It aims only to please, and while it does not always do that, it did so last night after having had an overhaul. The short play-story, however, was rather childish.

I think that review was a good example of being damned by faint praise!

In spite of this, however, my parents decided early on that television was going to be 'a good thing', and so one Tuesday afternoon during May, a 14-inch Sobell, on hire from Rentaset (later taken over by Radio Rentals), was installed in our living room in Pendower Way. On Coronation Day itself, we had a houseful of guests, neighbours and family, all crowding around the small screen to watch the event. My mother provided copious cups of tea and sandwiches and cakes for lunch. The rain poured down all day, so our party was indoors, as were all parties on that momentous day.

Douglas Bond

There was a big shift from radio to TV. We got our TV because of the Coronation like a lot of people. My mother was always trying to keep one jump ahead. Most of our relations got a standard model with a 9 inch screen. They had a nice clear picture but you had to get in close. My mother got a huge cabinet with a 21 inch screen. It was like a flat cinema screen with the cathode tube inside it that projected up onto the screen. You got a big picture but lousy definition. You still listened to radio a lot.

John Steel

In the evenings we listened to the Home Service on the wireless – Jimmy Edwards in *Take It from Here*, the Light Programme, and more rarely the Third Programme, and to records bought at Windows. Television had hardly arrived; my grandmother had a small

NEW TELEVISION TUBES FITTED

12 MONTHS GUARANTEE
*
48 HOUR SERVICE

12" — £10
14" — £13
17" — £15

Cash on completion

Always a small quantity of used sets in stock.

Mr. H. J. ORD.
T.V. Agent.   Tel: Gosforth 51288.

The cost of buying and repairing television sets was high. It might cost an entire weekly wage for a new tube, so renting was very popular. Or there was the never-never. In 1959 you could buy a set for 14s 6d a week over two years (a huge sum of over £78 in total).

Below, a 1958 schedule.

TODAY'S TV

5.0 — Children's Television: Pepe Moreno, Look.
6.0 — News Summary, Sports News, Weather.
6.9 — Regional News.
6.20 — Dale Robertson in "Wells Fargo."
6.45 — Tonight with Cliff Michelmore.
7.23 — News Summary, close of play cricket scores.
7.30 — Wish You Were Here at Llandudno with Peter West.
8.0 — Sid Caesar Invites You.
8.30 — Television Playwright presents Michael Denison in "The Inside Chance."
9.45 — A Double Date with Ken Morris and Joan Savage.
10.0 — News and Behind the Headlines.
10.20 — Celebrity Recital with Yfrah Neaman (violin) and Howard Ferguson (piano).
10.45 — Speaking Personally: Viscount Stansgate.
11.0 — News Summary.

Tomorrow afternoon

2.30 — Lunch time cricket scores.
2.32 — Watch With Mother.
2.47 — Mainly For Women.

one, black and white of course, which had been bought for the Coronation and was kept in the dining room. But telly was on its way – later I used to go to an aunt's house to watch *Emergency Ward Ten*.

Jane Jantet

When we got our first TV, I remember rushing home from school, Mam plugging it in and then sitting waiting for the valves to warm up and then the wonder of wonders – the test card! On children's TV there were the Wooden Tops with Spotty Dog and Muffin the Mule, with strings showing! Then on to *William Tell,* Roger Moore in *Ivanhoe* or Richard Greene as *Robin Hood*. When all the programmes finished they played the National Anthem and showed a picture of the Queen, a voice would say 'Goodnight' then everything was black apart from a tiny dot in the centre of the screen which gradually faded as the tubes cooled down.

Pat Rogerson

As an eight-year-old in 1955, I struggled with my mother, trying to get to the front of the crowd in the Co-op store on Newgate Street to watch the FA Cup Final on a small black and white television set. What a day that was! There were crowds such as I had never seen before, in the shop and outside in the street. Everyone was ecstatic at 4.50pm as Newcastle United lifted the cup. I know that the Co-op sold four television sets that day, so they were as happy as everyone else.

Tom Smith

A TV station for the North East

In October 1958 Tyne Tees Television was announced by the Independent Television Authority. It hit the airwaves on 15 January 1959. Adrian Cairns introduced the Duke of Northumberland at 5pm to launch the station before the rest of the evening continued:

5.15: The Adventures of Robin Hood

5.45: Popeye

5.55: ITN News

6.05: North East News

6.15: Prime Minister Harold McMillan interviewed live.

6.25: Strange Experiences

6.30: Highway Patrol

7pm: Big Show (opening extravaganza)

8.00: Double Your Money

8.30: The World this Week

9.00: Wagon Train

10.00 ITN News

10.15: Murder Bay

10.45: Sports Desk

10.55: I Love Lucy

11.25: Meet George and Alfred Black (Directors of Programmes)

Epilogue

In 1958 the new Tyne Tees Television premises were going up on City Road. December's 1958 What's On guide noted 'A low power test signal has been radiated from a temporary aerial half way up the mast at Burnhope for some weeks past.' In March 1959 a new live show from the studio was announced in What's On: The Bobby Thompson Show. Wor Bobby would appear with his wife Phyllis and a cast of eight every week, and 'it is hoped that the secretary and steward of a real Working Men's Club will be able to take part'.

What's On for January 1959 announced: 'Tyne Tees Television. The Consett Citizens Choir, under their conductor Mr. W.C. Westgarth, has been booked to appear in the big opening show on Thursday, 15 January. The Musical Advisor (Mr. Dennis Ringrowe) says "They will be the George Mitchells of the North East". Music for lunchtime programmes will be provided by an instrumental quartet led by Dennis Ringrowe on piano.'

Great Balls of Fire

Jerry Lee Lewis, 1957

Give us a tab then!

everybody did it. It was the done thing. Film stars did it best and died of it. Humphrey; Lauren; the Duke in *The Quiet Man* did it like a mad thing crossing those Irish fields on his way to fight Victor McGlaglen for the love of Maureen O' Hara.

'Look at the size of the dumps he's hoying away man. Aa wish aa was following him,' came an envious cry from the row behind in the Brighton Cinema. The screen could barely be seen for the smoke making pretty curling patterns in the projected light.

I had my first 'tab' at the back door of St Augustine's C of E Church on Brighton Grove in about 1954 with a lad whose name I remember but couldn't possibly repeat. It was a Woodie, wouldn't you know, a Woodbine, a Wills Woodbine, small but perfectly formed to fit in a pocket. I never looked back except to cough a bit.

Everyone, smokers and non-smokers included (they got it free then but statistics showed they paid for it later) breathed the smoke into unsuspecting lungs. Clothes reeked of tobacco smoke, houses reeked of it, as for soft furnishings Pooh ! But we never gave a thought to it in the dragging in, blowing out, inhaling, exhaling, dog-end flicking, ashtray-filling 1950s.

Players Bachelors were the next temptation but were soon abandoned as a bit girly and I moved on to Capstan when in funds but returned to Woodbines, which were the tab of choice when pocket money was running low. Really posh were Churchman but these were generally only received as gifts.

The first thing you had to learn after lighting up in a force nine gale was not to 'fake it'. Only weaklings and the uninitiated did that. The real, tough as nails, stylish hard lads inhaled right down into the lungs and back through the nose in satisfying streams of the blue smoke. That was proper smoking, no mistake. It was a relief when the children were old enough to smoke legally. The problems for the unimaginative of birthday and Christmas presents were solved. You had cigarette cases, cigarette lighters, cases for cigarette lighters, cigarette holders (for the more effete), cigarettes themselves in wild abundance to choose from.

Art school students in Heaton, 1958, with cigarettes, of course (the essential accessory), and in black, of course.

There were some wonderful ad hoc places to smoke when a lad, the school toilets being a particular favourite. The appropriately named 'dog ends' of the Plaza, the Brighton, the Regal or the Embassy were good. The style was feet up on the seat in front, tab in hand, and puff away like a film star without an audience. I remember clearing snow and getting just enough to pay for a seat in the dog end of the Plaza and five Woodbines, one and threepence, heaven? Not really, the film was a stinker called *Emergency Call* featuring the then ex-boxer Freddie Mills. Five Woodies was going it a bit on a Monday night when paper-round money was blown. The usual was a single cigarette bought at the Midget Shop for twopence. We knew how to live in those days.

In times of poverty a single tab could be passed between three or four lads. In my peer group the rule was three drags each and hand it over to the next man. By the time we reached the school gate we were ready to face the day.

Not everyone approved of smoking of course. There were dire warnings of stunted growth and shortage of breath but although the breathlessness affected many of us, the lack of growth was never proved to my satisfaction. I might have reached six foot instead of a very average five foot ten. Nobody approved of nicotine-stained fingers as far as I can recall but there were plenty about. They went with nicotine-stained moustaches and roll-ups. Roll-your-own tabs had that extra cachet of manliness. A baccy tin, Golden Virginia or Old Holborn, some Rizla papers and you were up there with the lads. The real experts treated machines with contempt and became adept in hand rolling, adding a fascinating level of loucheness that ready-mades quite lacked. I often wondered how much tobacco was lost in the learning process. Might have saved some lives.

All this was going on mostly in an 'ignorance is bliss' way through the Fifties, but a scientist named Richard Doll had already stopped smoking as a result of his findings and published a paper in the *British Medical Journal* linking smoking with lung cancer in 1950. In 1954 the government gave out advice that the relationship between smoking and lung cancer had been established.

But did we know or care? Well, not until much later as far as I was concerned. Along with millions of others I continued to puff away until the 1970s. Lots of us still haven't learned.

Michael Young

Smoke city

Newcastle was GREY! Dirty streets, black stone buildings, and smelly clothes especially on buses when it was wet. Smoke everywhere from factories and domestic chimneys, everything was covered in soot. And when it rained, a black slime on the pavement. The River Tyne was an open sewer. There was a fug upstairs on buses that you could cut with a knife. I started smoking when I was about 15, it just seemed the thing to do. Adults passed their cigarettes round, it was a social custom. All the movie stars smoked and everyone smoked in the cinema too, little red dots in the dark. Cigarette ends and ash all over the place.

John Steel

Traffic on the Tyne Bridge, 1959.

We travelled by bright yellow silent trolley bus, or on the purple motor bus with its ubiquitous exhortation to Shop at Binns, or as a great-aunt used to say 'Binns…s…s'. We'd be wreathed in smoke if we went upstairs. You could hardly breathe. Everyone smoked, Craven A, Senior Service, Players, Woodbines – no cancer scares then – and although we didn't realise it, everything smelt of smoke. Jane Jantet

To travel by public transport in the 1950s – and most people did as car ownership was beyond many – was to risk asphyxiation on a daily basis. Smokers, and there were lots of them, were allocated the upstairs of double decker buses. You only had to climb halfway up the stairs for the fug to catch the back of your throat with a peculiar kind of sharpness. Tony Henderson

Cough, splutter

In the 1950s everybody smoked like mad, or at least that is my lasting impression of the era. The fact that we were harming ourselves by polluting the environment didn't matter tuppence, pollution was a fact of life in the industrial north. Besides smoking was more than inhaling nicotine per se, it was part of popular culture. It was a passport to sociability; we started to smoke because our peers and friends smoked before ever becoming addicted. Smoking together was always more fun than smoking alone.

Wherever the public congregated there was smoking. Non-smokers were unsociable just like non-drinkers in a bar. Restaurants, cinemas, theatres, public transport, pubs and clubs all surrendered to the demands of the smoker, with only token gestures of consideration for non-smokers. If you went to the 'pictures' the cinema was more likely than not polluted with cigarette smoke and ash trays were provided on the back of every seat. When the lights were dimmed you could see hundreds of lighted cigarette ends darting about in the gloom like so many glow worms in the night. If you went to the doctor's the waiting room reeked of stale cigarette smoke and more likely than not the doctor was chain smoking with an overflowing ash tray of stubs on his desk and nicotine stained fingers!

There were literally hundreds of different brands of cigarette and the brand a man smoked and his smoking style absolutely typified him. The working man could only afford Woodbines, which came in paper packets of five. To make them go further he would nip them and light them again later. Those with middle class pretensions smoked Players or Senior Service, which came in packs of 20, and were passed round amongst friends with pride. But only the 'toffs' could afford to smoke the best hand rolled brands such as the exotically perfumed Balkan Sobranie, or Lambert & Butler or the distinctive oval shaped Passing Cloud, often through a cigarette holder held in a gloved hand and smoked with a style and elegance that could only be wondered at.

The persuasive powers of cigarette advertising in the 1950s are not to be underestimated. There were even cigarettes that claimed to be beneficial to the health, especially recommended to those of delicate disposition and sold at certain chemists. Cork and filter tipped cigarettes were preferred by the ladies and my mother went for the menthol flavoured brand, which claimed to be harmless and were like smoking toothpaste but a lot more dangerous. She called them mountain streams, which illustrate the powers of persuasion of cigarette advertising. Even I was not immune and when I attended classical concerts at the City Hall I carried a pack of Players No. 3, a more expensive brand with the distinctive white packet and gold lettering to boost my image as we casually stood smoking on the staircases during the interval. The cigarettes cost me more than the seat for the concert!

We didn't realise then that we were all smoking ourselves to death. Had we known, however, I wonder if it would have made any difference. In the 1950s we were still recovering from a dreadful world war that had spared no one and we all felt lucky to be alive but looming in the distance was the very real threat and horror of total extinction by something even more powerful than the atomic bomb as the Cold War intensified. There was a time to smoke and time not to smoke and that, in the 1950s, was yet a long way off.

Joe Pegg

When I reached 21 my presents included a cigarette case, a cigarette lighter and a large box of Senior Service cigarettes. It seems I was expected to act like a man, with smoking being a major part of that process. Another gift was a trilby hat (which I rarely wore) in the days when most men wore some sort of headgear. A few months later, following success at a local tennis club tournament, my prize, believe it or not, was a box of 100 Players cigarettes probably worth about £1. I never enjoyed smoking, never could afford it when young, and never became addicted. My smoking career was brief, though on one occasion at the Empress Ballroom, Whitley Bay, I broke all records by lighting up three times in one evening … I must have been bored!

Alan Morgan

Oh Happy Day

Don Howard, 1952

The Coronation, 2 June 1953, and the Queen's visit, 29 October 1954

1953 saw the grandeur and the pomp of the Coronation of Elizabeth II. Very few houses had television but many people bought sets in order to view the ceremony – only black and white of course, and tiny compared to today's standards. I invited a dozen students to come and join my uncles and aunts, all of us crowding round this miniscule set and eating sausage rolls and sandwiches. We had a wonderful day.

Elizabeth Sefton (née Whitfield)

I was born the week after the Coronation, the first of six children. My late mother had the distinction of being the first person in the street to buy a television. It was bought specifically for the Queen's Coronation and on the big day our front room was packed with neighbours who contributed something to eat and drink. They all sat glued to the tiny screen in the corner of the room. We always had a television from that day but we children were only allowed to watch after tea for one hour then we were sent to bed. The only programmes I can remember are *Robin Hood* starring Richard Green and the *Buccaneers* starring Robert Shaw.

Lynn Steele

ncjMedia Ltd

Grey Street, dressed for the Coronation, June 1953.

Newcastle went to town over the Coronation celebrations. Trolley bus poles were painted purple and sported crowns on the tops; nearly 300 hanging baskets of flowers brightened up Grainger Street, Northumberland Street and Grey Street; and four special buses (above) were decorated (including three double-deckers). The double-deckers would travel on different routes so that everyone would get the chance of a ride (at normal fare). The single-decker took part in the Lord Mayor's Coronation Show on 6 June. The vehicles were sprayed gold and decorated with the royal insignia.

We decorated our street to celebrate the Coronation. Dad took the shelves out of some cupboards and cut shield shapes out of them. He painted a red lion on each one and tied them to the lamp posts in Dissington Place. We never did replace the shelves.

Pauline Luke

Pine Street, Elswick, above, and Sycamore Street, left, prepare for the Coronation party, June 1953.

A paper merchant lived at the end of the street and he donated miles of red, white and blue crepe paper streamers. Everyone in the street went to our next door neighbour's to watch the Coronation on TV and we all crammed into their front room.

Pauline Luke

Elizabeth Street, Byker, cleans up the back lane in preparation for their street party. The walls seem to have been especially whitewashed. Parties took place all week all over the city. Unfortunately the weather that week was poor and, after 24 hours of continuous rain, 2 June's planned fireworks on the Town Moor with dancing and bonfires had to be postponed until the Saturday. In Bowman Street there was a red, white and blue archway complete with flags and portrait of the Queen and the residents planned a floodlit fancy dress party for 2 June (presumably it was rained off).

I went to the West End Boys' Club for the Coronation. They projected the TV images onto a big screen for us. And we were all dressed up to the nines. We stayed there all day – just as well because it was pouring down with rain.

Mary McArdle

For the Queen's Coronation our school decided to have a party and all the children had to come in fancy dress. My parents entered into the spirit of this and made mine and my brother's costumes. I went as Britannia complete with helmet, shield and tripod, and a white sheet doubled as my dress. My brother wanted to be a pirate. No Captain Jack Sparrow in those days, Long John Silver from Treasure Island (the wooden leg was a problem, so we did without) but he did have a tricorn hat, some old shorts, a wooden sword, baggy shirt and of course the black eye patch. We were all given paper Union Jacks to wave and a party tea. The Union Jacks always came

The Duke of Northumberland's coach passes two little boys in their best clothes on Northumberland Street.

in handy as we were often lined up on the route to the ship yard to wave to various royals who came to launch the ships. Occasionally we were allowed to go into the yards to watch the actual launch.

Pat Rogerson

1953 was the Queen's Coronation and I was chosen from the youth club to go to London as a guest of the Admiralty. A few of us travelled down by train and stayed in a hotel along Buckingham Palace Road. We paid a visit to the Admiralty, were taken on a boat down the Thames and given special seats in a stand near the statue of Queen Victoria outside Buckingham Palace.

Mary Dodds

As the great day drew near, thousands came out to view the decorations. Bainbridge's and Binns on Market Street entered fully into the spirit of the celebrations. Coloured lights were switched on on Grey's Monument on 31 May and stayed up until 15 June. Members of staff at Fenwick's enjoyed a special Coronation lunch given by the Directors on 1 June. There were flags just about everywhere.

When the Queen came to Newcastle on Friday 29 October, 1954, I was three. The royal cars came up Osborne Road past our house on their way to the Mansion House. There were kitchen chairs outside on the pavement for children to stand on, and we had flags at the ready to wave. I remember her going by, waving from the back window of the black car ... but she didn't wave or look at ME! I was most put out, and after all the excitement it was over in a flash.

Anna Flowers

Elizabeth Clark

Student Elizabeth Thompson (later Clark) captured the crowds in Northumberland Street on 29 October 1954, when the Queen visited on her Coronation Tour. Security doesn't seem to have been an issue!

Little Things Mean a Lot

Kitty Kallen, 1954

Polio House

While I was in the army in India in 1945, I contracted Infantile Paralysis, now known as Polio. In 1948 I founded the Newcastle & District branch of the Infantile Paralysis Fellowship, which soon became the most successful in the UK due largely to the generosity and physical help of the local people who, like me, were volunteers.

Known as the 'Summer Disease,' there were many sufferers from Polio back then and it was not until the late 1950s that the Salk Vaccine was administered nationwide to children. In the early 1950s there was still severe rationing and towns and cities were recovering from bombing and wartime deprivation. I soon discovered, especially in the poorer areas of the city and outlying areas, Polios living in completely unsuitable conditions, parents, who had no idea how to help their children, an emerging NHS, a very limited public transport system and practically no thought or time for the disabled. Against this background I also discovered how generous and compassionate the people of the North East could be.

In those days disabled people were not expected to travel far but in 1951 I organised a visit to the Festival of Britain, an enormous undertaking. Thirty-four Polios and eight helpers boarded the sleeper train to London and I can still hear the shrieks of laughter as callipers were removed and efforts made to get into the narrow bunks as the train set off! For two days the Metropolitan Police provided a motorcyclist to escort our special coach, we ate at Lyons Corner House and visited The London Palladium.

While volunteer help was always welcome, the branch was basically run 'by Polios for Polios' and this gave many, who had previously just sat at home, a new lease of life. Even the most severely disabled were given things to do, like manning a door, filling envelopes and sticking on stamps. This helped them to develop a sense of purpose and self-esteem.

It had always been my dream to establish a specially adapted hostel for Polios where they could live and learn a trade, so I applied to the King's College (now Newcastle University) 1954 Rag Committee for help towards this aim. They decided to donate the whole of the proceeds, which eventually amounted to £13,322 – a huge sum in those days. With this money I bought a large house, No. 1 Lindisfarne Road, Jesmond, and converted it to house 20 sufferers. It became famous throughout the country and Europe as it was the first of its kind in the world. On 22 September 1956, my dream was realised when it was officially opened by the Lord Mayor of Newcastle. The hostel, with its ramps, sliding doors, low-level handles, wash basins and switches, central heating, hoists, lift and banana slide fire escape, was revolutionary for the 1950s and brought valuable publicity, not only to the Fellowship but also to the city.

Most importantly I established a work scheme to train both residents and local Polios in silk screen printing, fretwork, making animated collecting boxes and working a printing press. A wooden hut was built in the grounds, which eventually housed a Christmas Card Department employing 30 Polios. By 1959 it reached sales figures of over £150,000. To do this we needed telephonists, packers, dispatchers and office staff to do invoicing, banking and accounting. They were all paid a proper living wage and I thereby proved what I had always believed, that

Joseph Fisher

Polio house, top, and, above, Joseph Fisher with the Lord Mayor at the opening on 22 September 1956.

with a little TLC and minor adaptations in the workplace, those thought by some people to be unemployable were capable of proving their worth, earning a living and through this growing in personal dignity. This was an entirely new concept.

The need for the workshop and hostel decreased as many married or got jobs elsewhere. Fortunately, due to immunisation, there were no new victims of the disease so the house was sold to a Housing Association in 2009. The financial benefit to the Fellowship has been great but the benefit to

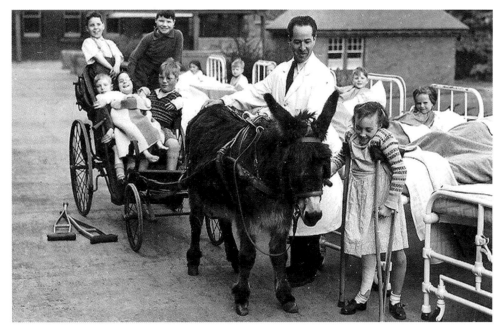

We had kind offers of help from all sorts of donors. One day I had a call from Lady Middleton of Belsay Hall to offer us a donkey and trap. Charley's Aunt (above) was the donkey's name and we stabled him in Kenton Lane. I would walk him down to the Sanderson Hospital on Salters Road for the children there.

On our first visit Matron remarked it was a pity the children who were too disabled to come down from the upstairs wards to the grounds couldn't see the donkey, so we put Charley's Aunt into the lift and took him up to the ward! The children were delighted. (I don't think Health and Safety rules would allow a donkey into a hospital ward nowadays.)

the past residents has been beyond calculation. Polio House was in action for over 55 years and has been a testament to the good work that the University Rag does. Without their help all those years ago, this story could never have been told.

Joseph Fisher

Puttin' on the Style

Lonnie Donegan, 1957

Shopping in the city

Many parts of old Newcastle were still almost medieval, but the city was beginning to wish itself into the modern world and that would come quite soon. Round the corner from Collingwood Street is the Groat Market and tucked into one of its ancient courtyards was an excellent shoemaker/cobbler. A plaque on the wall of his workshop declared that he was a member of St Crispin's Guild of Shoemakers and my, could he perform a miracle with a pair of ruined shoes.

During my lunch breaks I explored the Haymarket and Percy Street which remained as they had been since the beginning of the 20th century, except that the trams no longer ran. The Haymarket, beside the bus station, was full of small retailers selling clothes and shoes. Opposite, on the north side of the street there was a large cinema as well as the university book shop and several other shops and pubs. Percy Street looked very much as it had done for centuries with ancient, tiny-roomed shops fronting on to the street. Behind them were the old, crowded, cobbled courtyards. The small factories that had once been on the north side of the street had gone by the 1950s but the painted end walls still proclaimed the former businesses.

The Co-op store in Newgate Street was an elegant art deco building which was always crowded with eager customers. Elsewhere in the city there were other large stores including Farnons in Nun Street, Bainbridge's and Binns in Market Street, Fenwick's in Northumberland Street and Parrish's and also Beavan's in Byker.

Maureen Brook

Going exploring

Free time before my train home allowed the opportunity to explore the heart of the city for the first time. Murton's department store, where a tolerant salesman let me handle an extensive range of big game rifles, shotguns and fishing tackle, was a favourite haunt of mine. Alfred's toyshop in the Haymarket, was where I bought my first rod (I have it still). In Bagnall and Kirkwood I had a crush on

The Haymarket, 1955.

the assistant who was of indeterminate age with a glossy black pageboy cut, the same woman surely who manned the door of the Cavendish Club years later. MacFisheries next door put on a fascinating display. Strange junkshops nestled in cobbled closes, one particularly ancient one in Chillingham Road where I bought a faded copy of American *Field and Stream* magazine with the advert 'Nothing beats Springtime like a brand new Chevy' with an appropriate glamorous illustration.

Guy Hall

Murtons of Grainger Street advertises its men's range for 1951.

137

Mawson Swan & Morgan, Grey Street, decked out for the Coronation, 1953.

By the late 1950s, working and more affluent, I discovered the upmarket city of long-established family firms sadly now gone, such as John Moses and Isaac Walton's for smart fashion, Robson's and Harkers for furniture, and Mawson Swan and Morgan for books, art and leather goods.

Maureen Callcott

John Moses, Grainger Street, is on the right of this photograph from around 1948.

Mam's cousin used to work at John Moses. She'd done lots of make-up courses and did make-up in the store. She was married to a Frenchman and used to call herself Madame Angers. One day I went in for a facial and she used Chanel products. I kept wondering where I could go that night. I had nowhere to go, but didn't want to take off my posh make-up.

Mary McArdle

Blackett Street, looking west, 1955.

Newcastle had the largest and best stores in the region, which provided a Mecca for the more discerning shoppers who poured into town at weekends. I used to go to the town on a Saturday just to mingle with the shoppers and be part of the excitement. I bought my gramophone records at Windows or Alderson and Brentnall, or at one of the many other record shops such as The Wireless Shop or Jeavons on

Blackett Street around 1959, looking east. Tilleys is on the left, Burton's is the white building beyond. In the distance is Newcastle Central Library and the Laing Art Gallery.

Pudding Chare. Records then were still heavy, breakable and spun round at 78 revolutions per minute but the long player was being introduced. It played lightweight flexible records on a turntable that spun at only 33 rpm. I well remember with what fascination a crowd of us stood outside Windows Record Store in the Arcade watching a turntable revolving at 33 rpm in the window. No sound, just the turntable going round and round at a speed at which with a little training you could read the label on the record that was playing!

Joe Pegg

Swedish by design

In 1954, when I married a Swedish girl, I discovered a whole new world of double glazing, central heating, and good modern design in Sweden. Quite, quite different from 1950s Newcastle. Two years later I opened a shop called Lyktan (it means lantern) on Gosforth High Street, specialising in Scandinavian glass, lighting, china and gifts (I even imported some designs from a very new outlet in Almhult called Ikea). It was the first specialist shop of its kind in the UK, and a real hit. In 1961 we relocated to Grey Street.

Joseph Fisher

The shock of the new. Lyktan on Grey Street in 1961, featuring design from Sweden. Lyktan of Gosforth went down a treat in Fifties Newcastle. It was breath of fresh air.

The other side of shopping: Woolworth, Northumberland Street, in 1955, just before opening time. In the foreground is the household department with Brillo pads on sale at 2s 6d a box, whisks for 2s 3d.

Northumberland street in 1956. From the junction with Blackett Street shops on the left included: Burton's tailors, H. Samuel jewellers, Saxone shoes, Woolworth's, Fenwick's, Finlay's tobacconists, Boots the Chemist, Barratt's shoes, Jay's Furnishings, Lotus shoes, Summerfield jewellers, Mansfield shoes, Willson costumiers, Bewlay tobacconists, Etam's, Marks & Spencer, Martin's Bank, Freeman Hardy & Willis shoes, Dolcis shoes, M. & J. Taylor clothiers, Cowen gowns, Alderson furriers, Dampney paints, Lawson's sweets, Stephenson's sweets, Davison decorators, Hollingshead cameras, Armstrong sports, Jerome photographers, Alderson & Brentnall pianos, Green's bakers, Grafton's ladies' outfitters, Levene's wallpapers, Wilson & Carter's hosiers, Zip French cleaners, Maynard's sweets, Pegg dressmakers, Sutherland outfitters, and another Finlay's.

Northumberland Street, late 1950s. From the Haymarket, shops on the left included: Singer sewing machines, Finlay's tobacconists, Stocking Bar, Kirton's curtains, Southern butchers, Bookless fruiterers, Dictaphone, Henderson jewellers, MacFisheries, Glyn & Leinhardt furriers, Direct Raincoat Co., Bacon photographers, Paige Gowans costumiers, Cooper's butchers, Marcus furriers, British Home Stores, C&A Modes, Woodhouse furnishings, Richard Shops gowns, Callers furnishings, Audrey (Guinea Shops) gowns, Dodgson's, Robson's furnishers, Benefit shoes, Jackson the Tailors, Amos Atkinson shoes, Thomas Cook travel agents. There were two Carrick's restaurants, one was part of Queen's Hall Picture Theatre, the other was in the basement of the Pearl Buildings.

Growing up on Percy Street

I was born into a local family – well sort of, just before 1950. My grandparents escaped the pogroms and harsh conditions on the Russian/Polish border at the start of the 20th century. They settled in Merthyr Tydfil where they were married at the local synagogue, and, unable to find any work other than mining, my grandparents moved to Newcastle in around 1905 on the advice of friends from back home already settled up here.

My grandfather established what eventually became a successful clothing and tailoring business employing around 60 people at its peak, but the second world war put paid to all that as it did to many others. My father, however, decided that wasn't for him and in 1935, having already established trading posts around the North East, decided Newcastle city centre – the Metropolis – was the place to be.

He was astute, and in those days as today, footfall and an economic price were the major deciding factors in choosing a location. The one street that predominated was Percy Street – the gateway into the city from the Haymarket Bus Station. Northumberland Street, even in those days was still out of range, and better still the more reasonably priced Percy Street was without a jewellery and watchmakers' shop.

My earliest memorable visits were with my grandmother who lived at the family home, No. 54 Cavendish Place in Jesmond. She was a true matriarch who loved nothing better than to prepare lunch and then get the bus on Osborne Road with the meal in a wicker basket on one hand and me on the other, and off to town we would go. My

The Haymarket bus station around 1959.

father Lewis (Lewie) had been joined in the business by his two brothers Emmanuel (Manny) and Nathan (Natie). Once in town we soon arrived at the door of N. & L. Fagleman Ltd, 36-38 Percy Street, and as soon as I walked through the door I knew I was home. To have a wonderful father was one thing, but to be blessed with two equally lovely uncles was a true bonus. There was no better place in the world.

Percy Street in my early years in the 1950s became my second home. It was more a little village than a street – in fact it was my own little world. Our family shop was located around midway on the east side, further down from Handyside Arcade (where my father opened a second Percy Street shop pending demolition for Eldon Square) opposite.

Lewie and Manny Fagleman in the shop, 1959.

It was always a busy thoroughfare of pedestrians and of course shoppers. A good solid working- through to middle-class street, it was colourful and memorably odourful (not so good!).

My father's shop was of decent size and quite long. It was seldom empty. Opening hours were 9am to 6pm with the traditional Wednesday half day. To the right of my father's shop, going towards the Haymarket were first of all Maynard's, where I experienced my first taste sensation of the 1950s – a packet of Tudor Cheese and Onion crisps – the second best invention after the wheel! Then there was Teare's,

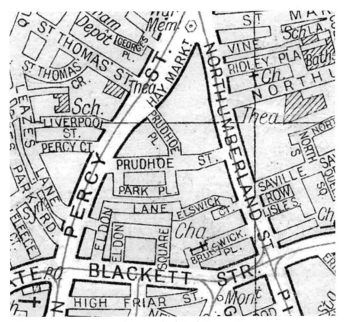

There was a maze of lanes behind Percy Street.

Prudhoe Street, from Percy Street. The Co-op is on the left hand side of the street, Prudhoe Street Mission is on the right, but not visible.

an antique and fancy goods shop, after that was Swinden's the cutler's with a gigantic pair of scissors, which sometimes moved with the aid of an electric motor, in the window. Thompson's the Pork Butchers, a fish and chip shop with red shutter (the smell of the old dripping was quite vile). Nearby was Grainger Boot Stores, where I begged my father to buy me a pair of winklepickers only to end up with the usual boring Oxford or Tuf shoes. Then there was Wright's, a drapery store that went round the corner ending up close to Bainbridge Hall, then round again to Prudhoe Street Mission and of course our local Co-op where I had to give our 'Divi' number and later get dividend stamps to stick in a little booklet.

The other way along Percy Street, heading south, was our neighbour the Pipe Hospital run by Chris McNeil. Around the corner in Eldon Lane was the 'Button King' run by the Adler family, upstairs from the Pipe Hospital. Across the lane was of course the Mecca for all children – Boydells, toy shop extraordinaire. The hours I must have spent staring in the window at all those Airfix kits and eagerly awaiting all the new Dinky and Matchbox vehicles to be on display. They never ceased to enthral me – what a shame I never kept hold of them in their original boxes, which of course went their journey not long after day of purchase – if only we could read the future.

On the corner of Eldon Lane, just yards from our shop, was the lovely Liza Sayers who had a barrow selling fruit, six days a week whatever the weather. She had four sons, Frankie, John, Peter and Albert and a daughter called Sylvia, a bonny young lady who worked with her. Our family were very fond of them and my father was always compassionate towards her as he knew she worked hard to support a large family. She sat by her barrow on a little stool with a small stove for boiling a kettle, which was always kept full by us. Nothing was taken for granted, any help she needed was on hand, and she always generously reciprocated with a nice melon or pineapple – luxuries in those days. I struck an immediate bond with her youngest, Albert who was the same age as me. We stood on that street corner for many years – there was always plenty to chat about as well as ready supply of fresh fruit, and that fruitful friendship has endured more than 50 years. My other buddies from those days still remain close friends – Terry Milligan who lived in St Thomas Street, and Peter Harker whose father owned Harker's Army Surplus Stores across the road on the corner of Percy Street and Leazes Park Road.

The Percy Street-Blackett Street junction, and Greig's empire of shops, around 1960.

Back on Percy Street, after Boydell's was Connor's – a

boot and shoe shop where my father took me in 1959 to buy a pair of hob nailed football boots and a tin of dubbin, prior to my starting Heaton Grammar school. Next door was Onion's, a shop that sold animal food, mainly for dogs. At the rear of the shop was an assortment of offal, off cuts and raw offerings scattered over the floor – tinned dog and cat food was not such a bad idea! Next to that was the next most odourful shop – Milburn's Shellfish Bar – a definite no-no to walk past on a hot summer's day before the bins were emptied. Next was Berry's, a small confectioner and

An utterly vanished view of the bend of Newgate Street with the Co-op far right, around 1955.

tobacconist and then Prudhoe Court. After that was a small parade of shops, called Greig's selling all sorts of clothing and drapery – almost Percy Street's answer to Harrods. Then came the local pub, the King's Head, where a little old newspaper vendor stood outside with his one leg and a crutch; we always bought our 3d *Evening Chronicle* from him. Crossing over Blackett Street, the shop on the corner was Milburn's, a pharmacy and also a bit of an apothecary's, much to the delight of my uncle Manny who was becoming a hypochondriac. I'll never forget the regular visits, particularly the one on which he acquired a bottle of Cascara Evacuant for suspected constipation. An over generous quantity of the recommended dose was taken and uncle was totally incapacitated for the rest of the week! Thereafter a cursory glance at the rogue bottle was an instant cure for the problem.

Back to the shop, I could go up and down the other side but one establishment 'out smells' all others. Waggott's Sheepskin Curing

Brian Fagleman

Brian age 10, 1959.

150

Warehouse was a true stinker, even more so because it was immediately opposite our shop. Daily wagons of sheep carcases, loaded up to the top and often overhanging, would drive up to the premises with its wide entrance and disappear inside. On a hot busy day the stench was so pungent that no one could pass by the premises – you had to cross over

Just at the corner of Percy Street, on the site of Barclay's Bank, there survived a little row of very ancient shops including Norman Macdonald's antique shop, the old Apple Shop, and George Wilson's shellfish shop. They were demolished in the early 1960s.

the road and give them a wide berth. Vermin of all sizes thrived there and the odd visitor was no surprise in our shop. Nevertheless, this was all part of the rich tapestry of Percy Street. Towards the end of the following decade it rose out of the ashes like a phoenix – the old warehouses and offices of the Handyside Arcade became the 'Carnaby Street' of Newcastle. I opened my first business there. God bless Percy Street.

Brian Fagleman

Shopping local

I remember travelling shops. There was Olsen the fruit and veg man, who also sold Oxo cubes. He was Dutch and he'd come round late at night in his little van. Once his van broke down and he came on a bike to say the van wouldn't be out that day. There was also a travelling butcher and a fish man.

Pauline Luke

We had everything we needed in Byker, all within walking distance, so we very rarely had to visit 'The Toon'. We went to three cinemas regularly; the 'Bamboro' on Union Road, the Black's Regal and the Apollo and we also had a theatre called the Grand. There was a Police Station, a Fire Station and a public library on Brinkburn Street. On Shipley Street there was the swimming baths and the public wash house where my Mum would take our big washing and our Grandma Hedley's washing. You could buy anything on Shields Road. We had any number of chemists including Boots, Kerr's and Dennison and Graham's. There was every food shop imaginable including Carter's near Potts Street, which was probably the forerunner to Greggs, and Woolworth's where we bought sweets, broken biscuits and slab cake (oblong Madeira cake that was cut into whatever size the customer wanted).

The larger shops were Bevan's, Parrish's (department stores) and Gill's furniture shop. The smaller shops included, for men, Jackson the Tailor and Greenwoods, and for women and children, Pledgers. Timpsons shoe shop catered for all. Once you were fitted out in your finery it could be recorded on film at Milvain Studios, photographers.

Our favourite shop was Parrish's and our Grandma Hedley could always be relied on to get a supply of Parrish's 'checks' (gold coloured coins with cutaway edges) for any large purchases. A Saturday treat would be the whole family visiting Parrish's top floor restaurant for tea and toast and being waitress served. As you can see we had everything.

Hazel Nixon

The Provi (Provident) agent could give you, as an advance on repayment, a 'cheque' or ticket that could be exchanged for tokens to use as currency to spend in Parrish's. Other shops had their own systems. The money would be paid back to the Provi (with interest) in small weekly instalments. In times of hardship some would sell their tokens on for cash, but you'd only get, say, £15 for a £20 cheque, and you'd still have to pay back the Provi!

Margaret Bingham (née Molly Johnson)

152

Shields Road, 1950. Everything you needed was on the 'Road' (Shield's Road, Byker) or at the shop on the corner of most streets. Some streets even had a pub, such as the Dues Bar. No need for Fenwick's when we had two department stores of our own, J.T. Parrish and Beavan's. As for record shops, butchers, green grocers, fish shops, pork shops, drapers and so on, more than you could shake a stick at. All with the added benefit of plenty of gossip as you would always meet someone with a story to tell.

Visits to the Toon tended to be for trips to certain stores such as Rowland Blaylock's, Wenger's or Waterloo House to use up a 'half order' or 'ticket'.

Joe Rogerson

A Rowland Blaylock token or 'ticket'.

Corner shops

I was about four years old when my brother Tony cut my head with a metal coal shovel while using it as a bat during a game of cricket in our backyard. After a visit to Walkergate Hospital I was due a treat for being brave. Shopping in Scarborough Road was very convenient. One of the ground floor terraced flats in the middle of the street (No. 27 in fact) was a shop, and the proprietor was Mrs (Sarah) Thomson. The window onto the street displayed the goods and you entered through the front door of the house. The shop was on the left in what was normally a bedroom. My treat was a bar of Caramac from Mrs Thomson's, which must have been the size of a paperback book or that's how it seemed to a four-year-old.

Keith Nixon

This large corner shop on Shieldfield Green was earmarked for clearance in 1956.

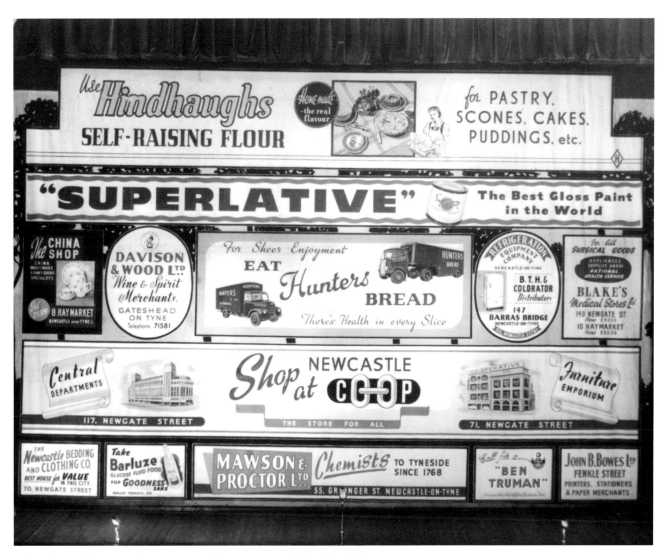

The Palace Theatre safety curtain advertises a wealth of local shopping opportunities in 1953.

Sweeties and other luxuries

One of the biggest disappointments for me when the war ended was that everything did not return to normal immediately. Reports of how well Germany was recovering prompted the common remark, 'You sometimes wonder who won the war don't you!' Rationing was still around for certain important items in the 1950s and, although there was plenty of propaganda on the upbeat Pathé Newsreels in the cinema about how much was being done to improve our lot and how the war spirit among the English people would help win the peace, there wasn't much evidence of it where we lived.

Joe Pegg

I walked for miles down Elswick Road to a shop that had Pontefract cakes with coconut on them. I got them and put the coupons back in my handbag. On the way home I realised that I had left the bag in the shop. I went back about ten minutes later and the bag was gone, with all the sweet coupons – two pages of them that were meant to last for a whole year. I was KILLED when I got in. I came home with nothing apart from the sweets I had in my mouth!

Mary McArdle

Rationing dragged on until 1954, and the last thing to come off was meat in July 1954 but more important to me was that sweets became freely available in February 1953. I had just turned 12 so it was a big deal. I rushed out to buy some.

John Steel

The end of sweet rationing in 1953 was more than welcome and my father and I set out for Fenwick's sweet department with a large carrier bag.

Elizabeth Sefton (née Whitfield)

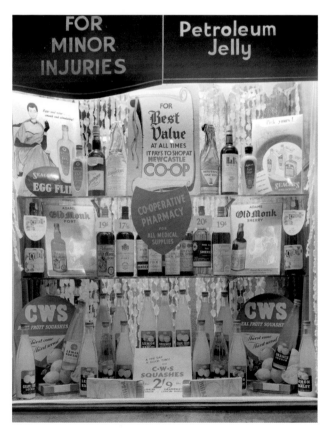

Co-op chemist, Welbeck Road, Walker, 1952.

Welch's factory in North Shields in around 1946.

Right, A Welch's sweet lorry heads the queue in this traffic jam on City Road at 9am one April morning in 1959. Traffic was being monitored as part of a traffic census. The first advertisement screened by Tyne Tees Television in 1959 was for Welch's toffee. Advertisers were charged £100 for 15 seconds during prime time.

She Wears Red Feathers

Guy Mitchell, 1953

Fifties fashion

We were, of course, an uptight, serious generation. We dressed formally – an outfit was not complete without a matching hat and gloves. Even in summer, white gloves were worn. Casual clothes were simply a lighter fabric, or a lighter-coloured cloth than was worn for work. No tee shirts, no jeans, in fact even the wearing of trousers for girls was a strictly casual form of dress; no 'lady' would have worn trousers to work. Nonetheless, after the dreary years of rationing, the world of fashion was now becoming much brighter and more plentiful. We had new man-made materials: celanese [rayon] or nylon underwear instead of brushed cotton and no longer in only peach or white, but in a variety of hues. Knitted bri-nylon cardigans in jewel-bright colours

Brian Sefton

A stylish wide-collared swing coat in blue-grey, with bracelet sleeves, is worn by Elizabeth Whitfield (seated). Her colleague, standing, wears a fashionable boxy jacket. Staff and students are enjoying a jazz concert from the roof of Newcastle University's Art Department, late 1950s.

could be tossed into the new electric washing machines instead of being hand-washed like woollen ones. Terylene skirts could also be washed instead of being expensively dry-cleaned.

Maureen Brook

In the summer of 1953 I left boarding school to come home to a new house in a hardly known town: Newcastle upon Tyne.

I was a 16-year old adolescent. Teenagers had not been invented and everyone's aim was to grow up, to have a long black cigarette holder and a little black dress, and go to cocktail parties. Clothes were important after years of school uniform. We had both summer and winter coats; I had a cream fine-wool summer coat with a standup collar that would look good today, and a heavy dark grey winter coat bought from Moses in Grainger Street, the most up-market department store in Newcastle, more select even than Bainbridge's, and sadly long gone. To go with it I had a mock patent leather bucket bag, which was all the rage. I also had a duffle coat and a black and white check mackintosh. We needed all those coats – central heating was rare and Newcastle was cold.

Duffle coat, Morris Minor, and a new fashionable haircut around 1955.

We had a lot of fun. We gave each other home perms, which came out frizzy and unmanageable. We went to parties in elaborate party dresses, and out of the office wore batwing sweaters and circular felt skirts with jaunty cotton scarves at the neck, and in summer New Look dresses, calf length, or with huge skirts held out by net petticoats.

Jane Jantet

When I was young I wore school uniform during the week, which I changed out of as soon as I got home. I had a tunic, a cardigan, a blazer, perhaps two shirts and two summer dresses. Most kids had a pair of good shoes and an older pair that were usually pretty battered and tight. I had wellington boots for the snow. I probably got a new pair of shoes every year. I always looked after my shoes, and polished them often, as I still do. I still have shoes that look good and are 20 years old.

I wore white socks in the summer and grey knee socks in the winter until I was about 14. There were no tights then. To go out somewhere special, visiting relatives, the cinema, and church, I wore my school blazer and my kilt: my parents were very proud of our Scottish heritage. I usually had a party dress that would last about three years. Clothes were bought with growth in mind. For school I wore a raincoat with a felt hat in the winter and in the summer a blazer and a panama hat.

There was a craze at school for trophy tassels on our scarves. The uniform scarf was a pale blue and navy stripe. The plan was to swap a tassel with your boyfriend, hopefully from the Royal Grammar School, as they had nice colourful tassels. Some of the sixth form had two or even three different tassels! Those of us who didn't have the necessary boyfriends raided our mothers' wool scraps and put a few tassels on our scarves. We were very naïve!

I usually got a new dress, sometimes a coat and the year's new shoes for Easter. This seemed to be a North East custom, as we found out when we opened our shop. But in my family's case it was because we always went up to visit our relatives in Glasgow for Easter.

Party dresses, white socks and slip-on shoes, 1956. I am centre with my first pair, and I was so proud! My friend, right, was much more sophisticated ... she had stockings and an older brother in the Navy who brought home records from America: Perry Como, Elvis Presley, Bill Haley and Gene Vincent. She also had a figure. Elspeth Rutter

At school we were supposed to wear our hats at all times along with the regulation navy blue knickers with a pocket in them. Two friends and I were disgraced by being made to stand out in front of the school at assembly and the whole school filed out past us. Our heinous crime was walking home from school with three boys and NOT wearing our hats. One of the boys was my friend's brother. However we were seriously letting the school down by our behaviour. Obviously I was wicked and out of control and was soon dispatched from this regime.

In 1958 I went to Art College. I was 15. I felt sadly lacking in the wardrobe department that September and my burning desire was to have some clothes in black or purple as soon as I could. The choice of fabrics in the Silk Shop was small, mostly evening and bridesmaids' fabrics or stuff that my mother would like. There was no teen fashion, you wore the same type of clothes as your parents except they were in 'younger' colours. We were desperate to change this and be different, so we bought furnishing fabrics from Chapman's at the top of Jesmond Road. This was a very forward thinking store, they imported Swedish designs. So I got my purple trousers, these were cigarette shaped and very narrow. Of course after a few washes they were even narrower. I could hardly walk or sit – but, they were PURPLE! I was the envy of all my classmates! No stretch fabrics then!

My parents were a little surprised at my desire for black and purple clothes, but my mother was very pleased when I insisted on a duffle coat from the Army and Navy Store on Percy Street. It proved to be the cheapest and warmest coat I had ever been bought. By Christmas I had lined up a holiday job at the big Woolworth's store in Northumberland Street next to Fenwick's. After that I had Saturday jobs at a café on Market Street and shop work for Carrick's the bakers on the corner of Gallowgate. I only got paid a small amount, but it was a fortune to me, and helped with the college expenses. It also helped with my

All dressed up for a wedding, 1957. I had made my outfit and my sister's with bolero jackets and wired little feather half hats to match. I also had a plastic clutch bag. The height of style.

What the grown-ups were wearing. A dinner dance at the Assembly Rooms, February 1953.

quest for a completely different and acceptable wardrobe.

Along with the beatnik clothes, the girls all carried baskets and the boys had haversacks. We all had lockers but for some reason we carried our heavy glass jars of poster paints around with us, down town at lunch time (walking) and back and forwards morning and evening in our baskets. One friend who had 'slipped up', even carried her baby around in her basket. It would be sitting quietly beside her in a pub or café.

We didn't use handbags, if we went out in the evenings we had our baskets (and paints) or just a purse.

Elspeth Rutter

1952 heralded my arrival at King's College. We all yearned to be adult and sophisticated so I took up smoking, complete with a long black cigarette holder! To add to my air of elegance I bought a little black hat with a veil, which I wore at the front of my head. I wore suits that I'd bought from Jaeger on Grainger Street and another black and white check suit that came from Fenwick's French department.

Elizabeth Sefton (née Whitfield)

At art college in my duffle coat, with a friend. I was very proud of my boots which were a new fashion item, as opposed to snow boots or wellingtons. My non-art college friends thought I looked as if I worked at the dog track! Elspeth Rutter

There was a little shop called Vogue near the Central Station. My friend Sylvia's mother said, 'When you leave school and get a job, you can have your first week's wages for yourself. And after that you hand it over'. So Sylvia had her first week in an office and had her eye on a dress in Vogue. She used to go every night to look at this dress. So on the Friday when she'd been paid – about 27 shillings – she got it and took it home. And her mother said 'How dare you open your pay packet!' 'But you said …' 'I said I would give it to you, I didn't say you could open your pay packet'. After that Sylvia had to hand over the pay packet and she was given pocket money.

Norah Coombes

Jam session night at the New Orleans Jazz Club in Melbourne Street, Newcastle 14 November 1959.

I wore felt circle skirts, and I attached many layers of net to a nylon petticoat at the base of the hip yoke. The fashion was for very full skirts but without the bulk at hip level, tiny waist and full busts, and at that time I had the waist to go with it. I favoured the wide elastic belts, which were also in vogue and with the right kind of buckle were easy and cheap to make. We wore blouses that were always tucked into waist bands. Julie Barton

Weddings were expensive to attend, so my parents usually got a Provident Order to rig us kids out. They were normally for Wenger's or Roland Blaylocks in town. In the 1950s, all the women had costumes to wear for formal occasions, whether it was weddings, funerals or christenings. Usually it was the same costume with only the blouse changed; bright for weddings and christenings and dark for funerals. Gloves and hats were a must.

I remember my gran telling my mam that I had to wear a Liberty bodice for starting school. It was to be worn over my vest. The novelty was that it had suspenders for attaching your woollen stockings; needless to say I only wore it for one winter then never again. Navy knickers with a white vest tucked in were the uniform worn for PE.

Pat Rogerson

C&A was my favourite shop, especially the bargain basement. I remember buying my first coat with my own money there, it was emerald green and mother went mad because she hated green and she wasn't there to help me chose it.

Mary Dodds

Stockings were an expensive item in the 1950s. Silk stockings were the most expensive and lisle stockings were cheaper at about four shillings a pair. Most of us wore lisle.

Nylon stockings were just coming onto the market. If you knew an American or Canadian serviceman you might be lucky and get a pair. By 1950, however, most of the servicemen had been posted home. You could send away to Gibraltar where stockings were available for 15 shillings a pair, plus excise duty.

As a junior typist my wage was 35 shillings a week. Fifteen shillings of this was my pocket money. Bus fares to work, trips

C&A advertises, 1951.

to the pictures, clothes, possibly a magazine as a treat – 15 shillings didn't go very far. No nylon stockings for me!

There was, however, an alternative to stockings. Leg make up from the chemist was cheap. I saved even more money by making my own from calamine lotion and a few drops of Mam's gravy browning. My parents didn't approve so I had to slip out without them noticing my 'sun tanned' legs. It was chilly in winter and it washed off in the bath so it was never a perfect solution.

Mabs Taylor

My very first pair of nylons came from Holland. My husband went there with the Territorial Army and brought them back for me. I was surprised and thrilled because they were so hard to get hold of. They were strong compared to silk stockings and showed off your legs so much better than lisle. Unfortunately a click or snag spelled disaster as they laddered so easily. I tried to avoid this by treating my precious nylons with kid gloves – literally! I would put on my gloves before putting on my stockings so I didn't snag them with my nails, then stroke the stockings onto my legs.

Agnes Chilton

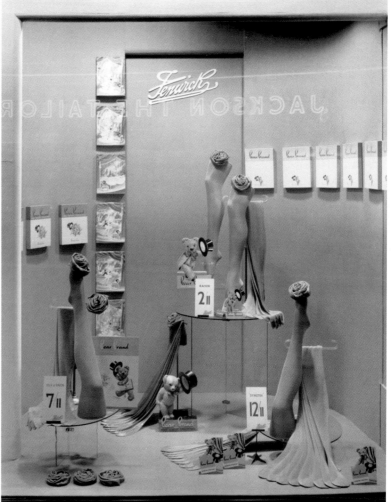

A display of Bear Brand stockings in Fenwick's window (opposite Jackson the Tailor), 1953.

When I worked in the drapery at the Co-op, I'd get nylons cheaper because I had staff discount. Even so they cost 4s 6½d. My sister worked at the laboratory at Wills [the cigarette factory, Coast Road] and was always asking me to get discount nylons for her workmates.

Carol Wilson

You used to wash your nylons every night and roll them in a towel to help them dry. If you got a ladder you could go to Fenwick's to get them repaired. There was a little girl who sat at a machine that picked up the stitch and reworked it. It cost about 6d a ladder.

Norah Coombes

You'd carry nail polish to stop ladders in your nylons. It would stick to your leg, but it didn't matter if it pulled the hairs on your leg when you took them off! As long as the ladder didn't go any further – nylons were expensive.

Mary McArdle

When I went for interviews (1956) I chose a bright coral coat from C&A, which was absolutely the only thing I bought during the year. I had a navy straw boater style hat, which had been a shabby second hand white, but I dyed it. I sometimes twisted a second-hand, long red and white checked silky scarf around it, leaving long ends trailing down the back. I seem to remember that I got it from the American exchange that ran during the war.

It was different in summer when I favoured sleeveless cotton dresses with net petticoats. I recall that spotted material was the fashion. At that time no 'respectable' woman went about without a hat and

C&A advertises, 1958.

166

gloves, even in summer, when the gloves were crocheted or net, usually white, but other colours were sometimes worn. The little so-called half hats were the vogue, but everyone wore headscarves, even the Queen. Other styles in favour were narrow skirts, coats with loose swinging backs, waist hugging jumpers and flat ballerina shoes.

My best outfit was a grey suit with a nipped in waist and a choice of two skirts, one pleated and the other straight, which my mother had funded for interviews.

Julie Barton

Advert from The Journal, 1951.

Fifties fashion tips

We used to put sugar on our petticoats to stiffen them and make them stick out.

Sugar and warm water in your hair would help it keep its style.

A very thin solution of gravy salts would darken your legs if you didn't have any stockings. A fine line up the back would do for the seam.

Hairspray was very stiff, like shellac.

Everyone wanted cats' eyes like Gina Lollobrigida so we went to a theatrical make up shop.

You could buy blonde hair pieces to pin into your hair, or you could get a blonde streak done at the hairdressers.

Duster coats were in. They were lightweight edge-to-edge coats with big sleeves.

We bought shoes at the Co-op or Freeman Hardy Willis or Parrish's.

We used to look at all the Fenwick's windows even if we had no money. The windows on Northumberland Street were so lovely.

Pauline Luke, Mary McArdle,
Carol Wilson, Norah Coombes

Eve Brown, Northumberland Street, opened in 1956 to cater for the expanding market in women's fashion. Note the ashtray for cigarettes, a constant companion when shopping.

Young Men about town

I arrived in Newcastle to study at King's College in October 1956. Although still very much an industrial city, it was much less polluted than my home city of Bradford and after the first year I chose to spend vacations in Newcastle. The Students' Union at that time organised Saturday dances (known as SNEC Saturday Night Entertainment Committee) in the Union building, but during the vacations we gravitated to The Oxford dance hall in New Bridge Street. Whereas informal dress was acceptable for SNEC, and jive was permitted – in fact almost obligatory – dress standards at The Oxford were more formal and respectable and jive was actively discouraged. So my friend Peter and I decided that if we were to make an impression there we needed to have suits. But with severely limited funds how were we to afford such sartorial extravagance?

Then one day we were passing by one of Jackson the Tailor's shops and were delighted to see that they were having a sale of suits at ridiculously low prices. Fifteen minutes later we

'What's happening to me?'

'I've always thought I was as easy to please as the next man, Mr. Jackson,' said this young fellow. 'But something seems to have come over me since I got that suit from you.'

'Why should that be, I wonder?' I said, smiling.

'Well,' he said, 'it was so much better than anything I'd ever had before, that it made me dissatisfied with the rest of my clothes. I found myself buying smarter shirts and ties—being particular about shoes. Then the chaps where I work began coming to me for advice, and treating me as if I was a senior.

What's happening to me?'

As I told him—something to be pleased about. His standard of dressing has gone up. I've seen it happen over and over again with our customers. We introduce them to suits with our own special cut and the rest follows. What a gain it is —in confidence, progress towards success, popularity in the office and out of it! Think I'm exaggerating? Come to us for your next suit—and watch it happen to you.

Prices (to measure or ready tailored) 8, 10 or 12 gns., and you can pay 'out-of-income' if you prefer it.

Jackson the tailor

left the shop each clutching a brand new suit. Saturday evenings were going to change for ever! Back at the house we rented in Chester Street, off Sandyford Road, we tried on our new purchases but were dismayed to notice that the front of each suit was several shades lighter than the back. This was glaringly obvious in broad daylight but had not been evident in the dimmer lights of the shop. Clearly they had been part of a window display and had faded in the sunlight. That's why they were so cheap.

Undaunted we decided that we would nevertheless attempt a foray to The Oxford. This, however, necessitated keeping to the darker corners of the ballroom and, instead of marching boldly across the room to accost a prospective partner, we sidled round the edge, keeping our backs as close to the wall as possible and thereby missing the best opportunities.

Nevertheless, once dancing 'cheek to cheek' in close contact with a partner our two-toned attire was well hidden. We avoided more open dances such as the Gay Gordon's, which we didn't like anyway, and were even pleased that we weren't allowed to jive.

Medical student Margaret Slater (now Bishop) with a group of snappily-dressed Norwegian exchange students in 1956 on Northumberland Street, just outside Fenwick's, opposite Jackson the Tailor.

Eventually we realised that people didn't really notice and we lived happily with our semi-faded suits for several years.

Brian Sefton

My first going out clothes were pretty close to teddy boy really. In the early 1950s, up to age 15 or so, you'd wear grey trousers and a white shirt, like your dad. But by age 15, everyone was discovering teenagers. The older ones had jobs and money and they could go and buy their own suits. They'd go to Burton's or Jackson's and have a suit knocked up.

Originally the teddy boy look was quite smart. The young guys were dress conscious and looked pretty cool but it got more outrageous as American country and western styles came in with curved pockets and ridiculous ties. The English look had velvet collars, turned back cuffs, covered buttons, and narrow trousers. But it morphed into the joke teddy boy look with brothel creeper suede shoes, and string ties, a combination of country and western and Edwardian. The Italian look came in too at the end of the 1950s, very smart. So we were junior teddy boys out on the town.

It was also the start of the beatniks, identified by the duffle coat (camel coat for trad jazz and navy or black coat for modern jazz) and polo neck.

Me and my friends were in all the gangs … cool, jazz, teddy boys, beatniks. I loved it! We could move between all the tribes.

Girls were wearing pencil skirts, sweaters, pony tails, and they wore Ava Gardner or Audrey Hepburn haircuts. There were plenty of jobs so youth had spending power and disposable income.

City Stylish sold the teddy boy and the country and western stuff. Marcus Price was more stylish, more tasteful. He came into his own with the Italian look in the late 1950s. In City Stylish you could get the Billy Eckstein Collar and the Frankie Lane collar, and gambler type bow ties with tails on. And fancy gamblers' waistcoats in shot silk. I had one of those.

On the beach at Scarborough in 1955 wearing a sharp suit.

John Steel

Marcus Price of Percy Street

Percy Street in the 1950s was an incredibly interesting part of Newcastle even though it was not a major part of the centre.

From the Haymarket to the Gallowgate turning, you had a series of small and extremely active businesses including the Pram Shop and Mark Toney, who are still in Percy Street today. Then the Levy brothers store and Steel's wool shop. There was a tool shop, known as the scissor shop because it had a massive pair of chrome automated scissors in the shop window. Next was Kiddy Kot, a children's clothes shop. Then on to the Pipe Hospital and the shellfish shop owned by a Mr Ephraim, who lived above the shop. Hearing burglars breaking into our shop, he reported it to the police who came and caught them.

Across the road was a small terrace of old stone-built shops with a cobbled corner before the pavement. The one I remember was an antique shop belonging to a Mr Macdonald and his son. It became the new Barclay's Bank. Then there was the original Harker's ex-army store and Aynsley's, a building materials and hardware store. Between them and our shop was an animal skin business, which stank on a hot day in summer. Next to our shop was the record store belonging to Mr and Mrs Jeavons, this was excellent for popular music especially jazz and blues. After them was a Halford's and the famous bike shop Herby Ray's and lastly the Three Bulls' Heads pub. It was a very down-to-earth street.

The Percy Street shop was opened at Christmas 1953, and I joined it in January 1954 after two years in the army. The plan devised by my father was to have a shop catering to a youth market, say teens to twenties, because these customers were only catered for by one shop, City Stylish.

A lot of fashion influences came from America, pop music, jazz, the blues, ice hockey, magazines such as *Esquire*, and of course record covers, especially ones by David Stone Martin.

The shop itself had a modern look; a shiny black glass fascia with our name

in large sharp red neon lettering, at one side is the logo of a man in a tails and cloak with a top hat – the very opposite of what we were selling. Within this arcade we had a lot of widow space and it was the window dressing where we really made our mark. We would dress as many as 40 shirts tightly on board formers and tie a tie and add cuff links. This took time but helped make our shops look different.

So what did we sell? We began with a mixture of old and new. The old, such as hats and caps along with two-collared shirts were the first to go. Our main features were, without doubt, shirts, shirts and more shirts. I think we were known as the shirt shop. They were all cut-away collars and took an extremely narrow tie known as 'slim jims'.

Some shirts were made from cotton but they were mostly rayon, which was called sharkskin as it was extremely shiny. These gave way to more cottons later.

In knitwear we had sleeveless cardigans and wool waistcoats with imitation ice hockey tops. They had a slashed neck with a two-tone stripe right across from one sleeve to another. We also did cardigans and light jackets in wool fabric.

Other clothing was somewhat sparse, but in the beginning comprised trousers in a number of colours in a rayon twill fabric – they tapered to a 14-15 inch hem with turn-ups. Jackets were an Irish tweed look in a pepper and salt black and white rayon

Marcus Price

Marcus Price

fabric. I must say these were improved upon in a few years.

The fashion trade moves quickly and by the later part of the Fifties we had moved on to some amazing products. We increased the size and refitted the shop to take in many products that were being boxed individually, such as the Sabre Saturday shirt made in Hartlepool. This was really a fine wool polo shirt. Most of the new shirts from new companies were being boxed. The range of shirts had widened and we were stocking more collar shapes, such as pointed and pin through and tab, which were very American looking.

In the late Fifties we had the opportunity of taking premises in the Groat Market and that was when we opened the Fifth Avenue Man's shop. It was a great extension to the business.

Marcus Price, Percy Street, around 1955. The sweater on the counter is a fashionable ice-hockey style design with a stripe down the sleeves.

Our customer base at this time was, to say the least, incredibly varied, but all had one thing in common – they were young. We have a lot to thank them for, as well as our excellent staff.

Marcus Price

Just Walking in the rain

Johnnie Ray, 1956

On the Road

After one of the Friday night dances at the Community Centre, I missed the last bus home so I had to walk down to Westmorland Road and wait at the bus stop near Rye Hill. That part of town wasn't very nice in the dark but as I was waiting a policeman approached and asked what I was doing there. I replied that I was waiting for the all night bus and he said 'it's not a nice place for a young lass to be waiting about in' so he stood with me until the bus came. It was smoky, noisy, full of drunks and I was a bit scared. I vowed I wouldn't do that again!

Northumberland Street buses crowd together at Cook's Corner, Northumberland Street on 31 March 1956. AEC Regent motorbus on route 2 is turning right into Blackett Street, while BUT 963IT trolleybus is on route 33A to Delaval Road. Another AEC Regent motorbus on route 8 passes on the inside.

This photograph was taken during a regular traffic census.

I remember the buses were cold and noisy but my most memorable journey to work was a ride on an open topped truck in the winter. I went for my bus a little earlier than usual, as the snow was quite deep and knew the buses would be running late. I arrived at the bus stop to find a number of people standing in the shelter, freezing cold and debating whether to go home or not. I would have lost pay if I didn't turn in, my mother would also give me a good telling off. So I decided to wait with some of the others who were in the same boat. A truck pulled up and the driver asked where we were going. He told us to jump on and he would get us to the town. So we did. When I got to the office I was soaking wet, freezing cold and late. The only means of drying off our outer clothing was to put them on the radiators, so that's what I did and we worked in a 'steam room' the rest of the day. The only concession we got was a hot drink!

Another time I had trouble with transport was when we went to Dudley to play table tennis. After the games we were given food and

Another traffic census in July 1956 shows a very busy Northumberland Street.

177

drinks and the time just flew over – consequently we missed the last bus. We didn't know what to do so I went to the local police station to see if they could help four girls in distress. A policeman said that apart from keeping us in the cells overnight, all he could offer was a lift in the van of a local man who was delivering some stuff in Newcastle. We thought we had better take up the offer! As we climbed in over cardboard boxes the driver said 'make your way to the back of the van', so we did, and one of the girls fell into the lap of man who was sitting there. We all screamed in horror but the policeman had seen what had happened. He checked who the man was and told him to behave himself! So we had an uncomfortable journey to Newcastle and the poor man in the back was terrified. What a telling off I got from my mother.

Mary Dodds

Despite a lengthy commute from Hexham to the Royal Grammar School in Jesmond, it was during my school days that my love affair with the city really began. At first it was a 'penny half, please,' tram journey from a stop opposite the Central Station to Jesmond. Trolley buses subsequently replaced these but still suffered from the same problem of the connection coming off the overhead wires. Reconnection was effected with a strangely old-fashioned bamboo pole. Leaping on and off at high speed was a favourite pastime, resulting in many a would-be passenger rolling over and over in the gutter as the angry shouts of the conductor gradually faded into the distance.

Guy Hall

Trolley buses turning into Neville Street, around 1950. Right, a tram token.

A No. 6 single-decker bound for South Shields inches into the traffic on Pilgrim Street on its journey from Worswick Street bus station, April 1959.

The now derelict Worswick Street bus station was the destination for south of the Tyne services. Its series of bus ranks were set on a perilous incline so wooden chocks had to be wedged behind bus wheels. The vehicles had to accelerate with a vengeance to escape the slope which meant clouds of noxious fumes constantly shrouded waiting passengers. Tony Henderson

The 1950s bus driver's badge was loaned by Brian Fagleman.

Traffic mounts on Pilgrim Street during the rush hour one morning in May 1959. The cars on the left are emerging from City Road as others turn into it. The buses ensured that nobody would ever forget to 'Shop at Binns'!

Morning and evening rush hours were chaotic, with most workers travelling by public transport. Bus services were many and frequent as can be seen from contemporary photographs, but even so bus queues were still a common sight.

I travelled to and from work by electric train. The platforms for the north of the Tyne east coast route were at the east end of the Central Station. Suburban trains were clean, reliable and frequent and stopped at all stations en-route, many of which are now closed. Tickets were purchased at the booking office and clipped by the ticket inspector at the barrier before boarding the train. I frequently had to stand for the full journey as the trains were so crowded.

Buses, both petrol and trolley buses, were boarded via a platform at the rear, under the supervision of a conductor, who was in absolute charge. Depending upon his fondness for

South Gosforth Station around 1955 with a Central Station bound four-car electric train, stopping at all stations from the Coast via Benton.

the rules, he would either cram you all in standing like sardines or declare 'Five only standing' and throw the rest off. Arguments and insults were exchanged between bus queue and conductor but any nonsense from passengers on the bus and the bus didn't move until it was sorted out. The conductor also set the tone on the bus with his or her cheerful disposition.

I had a good friend whose father was a bus driver and whenever he saw me walking to or from town he would slow down and shout for me to 'Hop on!' If he were on a route that took him past his home he would leave his bus at the bus stop dash down the street to his home, take his medicine and dash back to his abandoned bus and bewildered passengers and continue the journey. The worst bus service for being abandoned for long periods at the top of Heaton Road when changing drivers must have been the No. 19. I sat for over 20 minutes waiting for the next driver to take over. Years later I was casually flicking through Hansard when to my surprise I saw that the Newcastle No. 19 bus service and its problems had actually spread far beyond Heaton and Walker and had become worthy of discussion in the Houses of Parliament!

Joe Pegg

I Believe

Frankie Laine, 1953

Up for the Cup

My dad died when I was ten years old but I have lasting memories of him and my brothers taking me to St James's Park to watch Newcastle United. The whole family were mad Newcastle fans. In those days there was no seating, everyone stood to watch the match. The children could not see so we were passed down over the heads of the crowd until we were at the front behind the goal. I can remember having many a conversation with the goalies of the day.

On one visit the stadium was emptying after the game and dad sent my brother Brian to find me but I was nowhere to be seen. The police became involved and the grounds were searched to no avail. Dad and brothers Terry, Brian and John became worried they were going to have to go home and tell mam I was missing. Mam was called the Iron Lady long before Mrs Thatcher and was someone you didn't cross. One of the policemen looked up and shouted 'found him'. I had climbed up the flood light pylon which all the kids did but I had made myself comfortable on a ledge and fallen asleep. The first thing I can remember was one of my brothers carrying me down. I don't remember being told off. I think they were just relieved I had been found and they didn't have to face the wrath of my mam, May Steele.

Derek Steele

In 1951 I went with my father to Wembley on a football special train. Newcastle United were playing Blackpool and there was a big rivalry between 'Our Jackie', Milburn and Stanley Matthews from Blackpool. We won 2-0 and the FA Cup was ours. I shouted so much that I entirely lost my voice.

Elizabeth Sefton (née Whitfield)

Newcastle United won the FA Cup in 1951. I was there when they came home to the Central Station after their victory. Every Saturday afternoon the footballers arrived on the No. 4 bus to play the match. They'd go to the little Rendezvous café, next to the Odeon, for their dinner on a Saturday. They earned about £11 a week but only £7 in the closed season.

Joseph Luke

A match at St James's Park around 1950. You can just about hear the crowds roaring as the ball nears the goal!

I remember going with my father to the Central Station to see the team coming back with the Cup. I think it was a Wednesday,. To see the team on an open-top bus with the trophy was a great occasion for me and probably contributed to my lifelong passion for the game. You could not see Neville Street for the huge crowds outside the station and all the way up Grainger Street. Every street on the parade route was similar, and there was absolutely no room in St James's Park, which was full to the brim. Even Gallowgate and Barrack Road were closed to traffic. What a tremendous occasion.

Tom Smith

When I passed my intermediate accountancy exam in 1950, my weekly income rose from five shillings to £3 before deductions for tax and National Insurance. My new-found wealth meant I could widen my horizons within reason, and one of my first extravagances was a desire to be at Wembley Stadium for the FA Cup Final in 1951 between Newcastle United and Blackpool. I was very interested in football, having played on a regular basis for a boys' club until pressure of work and study became too great.

There remained the problem of how to obtain a ticket. When Newcastle United decided to operate a postal ballot system for tickets I decided that the only way for me, with no suitable contacts, was to get several relatives to apply by sending in a three shilling postal order (the price of a ticket) together with a stamped addressed envelope. Out of nine applications two were successful so Dad and I could make the exciting trip to the capital, where I had never been before. The rail journey was slow and tedious but once in London we saw many of the familiar sights as well as watching a superb 2-0 victory for United. The unsuccessful postal orders were all returned by the club.

Alan Morgan

Procter & Gamble

'Moonbeams', the Thomas Hedley magazine, featured NUFC's famous Jackie Milburn in 1954. A footballer's life was rather different in those days.

'Where do star footballers go in summertime? In the case of Newcastle United's Jackie Milburn – English International and scorer of the first goal in last season's Cup Final – the answer is that he concentrates on his one-man motor coach business. This summer he helped with the door-to-door distribution of Gleem samples on Tyneside by driving a Field Advertising team to many of their calls. This picture shows him lending a hand by keeping distributor Edna Oliver supplied with sample tubes.'

Many football heroes took jobs in the off-season. Some worked in Bainbridge's sports department.

The cup winners on their way from the Central Station in 1951, having defeated Blackpool 2-0. United were captained by Joe Harvey and Jackie Milburn scored the winning goals. George Robledo, Charlie Crowe and Bobby Mitchell were also on the team.

It was Friday 6th May 1955 and I was at the Central Station, Newcastle with my dad, Walter Dix. We were about to set off with the other 40,000 Newcastle supporters to see our team play Manchester City in the FA Cup Final on Saturday 7th May.

Newcastle were the FA Cup Final specialists having won in 1951 and 1952. Manchester had the revolutionary Don Revie and the famous Revie Plan to overcome us!

Dad, who was a shareholder in Newcastle United, had managed to get me a ticket. It would be my 13th birthday on 10th May so it was my special present.

The train journey down was full of fun with everyone singing and

In 1952 United defeated Arsenal 1-0 at Wembley. Joe Harvey (holding the cup) was captain once more and George Robledo scored the winning goal. Also on the team were Jackie Milburn, and Bobby Mitchell. The team returned in glory from the Central Station. Joe Harvey would retire on 1 May 1953.

laughing, with a few drinks thrown in. We were booked into a posh hotel near Marble Arch and after dinner, I was packed off to bed as we would have an early start the next day. Dad came in 'later'.

After breakfast we set off for Wembley on the Underground. Dad and I were kitted out with black and white rosettes and scarves, part of the vast army of support, a sea of black and white! THE MAGPIES! Up Wembley Way and up to the Stadium. Both sets of supporters walking up together, the blue and white mixing with the black and white, no trouble, plenty of rivalry and banter and a few insults but nothing nasty.

We were very fortunate because our seats were just to the right of the Royal Box. The bands played and the fans sang 'Abide with me' and the National Anthem to greet the Queen.

Then out came the teams, all my heroes. Three o'clock and the whistle went, then an amazing thing happened. Newcastle forced a corner. Len White took it and then from out of the players in front of the Manchester goal Jackie Milburn rose

Another glorious return for United from Wembley in May 1955 after beating Manchester City 3-0. Jackie Milburn, Bobby Mitchell and George Hannah scored the winning goals.

and headed home, after just 45 seconds!. My two football heroes. Jackie was not known for heading goals.

The game was fast and furious, Manchester equalized just before half time and then in the second half Newcastle got goals through Bobby Mitchell and George Hannah. We had won the Cup 3-1. Jimmy Scoular, the captain, led the team up to the Royal Box to receive the FA Cup from Queen Elizabeth. The cheers and excitement as they paraded the Cup around the pitch were stupendous. *The Blaydon Races* echoed round Wembley Stadium. The singing and dancing continued all the way down Wembley Way to the station.

Dad obviously knew we would win. He had booked a table at a very swish restaurant in Soho and then seats at The London Palladium for a variety show with Benny Hill, lots of singers and dancers, some with very little on! Then it was back to the hotel, passing lots of Newcastle supporters still celebrating. Dad got me to bed and said he would see me later as he had 'to see a man about a dog'.

A wonderful birthday present and one that I have never ever forgotten, especially as Newcastle United have not won a domestic trophy since!

Malcolm Dix

The winners return from Wembley, 1955.

Everything stopped for the winners' parade, 1955.

A little flutter

Like most working men my dad enjoyed a little flutter on the horses or dogs. There were no betting shops close to where we lived on Scarborough Road, Byker, but in our back lane on the Benson Road side there was an unofficial bookmaker. My dad always signed his betting slip RAFA (Royal Air Force Association) as he was in the RAF during the war.

Sometimes Dad would take my brothers, Tony and Keith, and me to the dog racing track at Brough Park. As we were all under nine years old we were small enough to be lifted over the turnstiles. We were quite happy collecting discarded coloured bookmakers' tickets from the ground while Dad was standing watching the races. Once at home the competition would be to see who had collected the most tickets of each colour.

Everyone was happy even if Dad lost, he would just laugh it off. He was a good loser!

Hazel Nixon

GREAT SPORT—
GREYHOUND RACING
AT THESE THREE
LEADING STADIUMS

More people are patronising these stadiums because they offer all that is best for sporting and social entertainment. Tip-Top greyhounds, first class organisation and excellent totalisator facilities ensure good sport, while the congenial surroundings of very good clubs and snack bars guarantee an enjoyable evening.

GOSFORTH STADIUM

EVERY MONDAY AND SATURDAY

BROUGH PARK

EVERY WEDNESDAY AND FRIDAY

GATESHEAD STADIUM

EVERY TUESDAY AND THURSDAY

FIRST RACE AT 7-15 P.M.

SPECIAL BUS SERVICES

Northern, United and Venture Bus Companies operate special buses from all parts to and from the Stadiums. An all inclusive ticket at 4,6 covers the return journey and admission to the Stadium. Ask for details at your nearest Bus Station.

FIRST CLASS RACING UNDER N.G.R.C. RULES

Y.M.C.A. Blackett Street
GYMNASIUM

Weight-lifting Club.

Meets for training on Monday Wednesday, and Friday evenings at 7.30 p.m.

Judo Classes.

Every Friday evening. Instructor: Mr. George Bamford.
(Black Belt)

Basket Ball.   Apparatus Work.

DINING ROOM.

Luncheons, served to Members, daily from 12 noon to 2.30 p.m.

TELEVISION.

Large Screen T.V. in the Buffet each evening.

SWIMMING CLUB.

Members meet every Monday evening at Northumberland Road Baths.   Beginners Welcome!

MOTOR CYCLE AND CAR RACING

10 May — Ashington Motor Club.
Motor Cycle Scramble at Ulgham Manor Farm, Nr. Morpeth at 2 p.m.

18 May — Seaton Delaval Club.
Grass Track Racing at Plessey Checks, HARTFORD at 2 p.m.   Racing for Motor Cycles, solo and sidecar, and for scooters.
Admission 2/- (children 6d.)   Free Car Park.

24 May — Gateshead Motor Club.
Grass track meeting at Hedley on the Hill, Nr. Greenside.

31 May — Newcastle & District Motor Club.
Sand race meeting at Druridge Bay beginning 2 p.m. Admission free. Car Park Charge. "United" will run special 'buses. Proceeds from the Car Park will be in aid of the British Empire Cancer Campaign.
Border Racing Club.
Next meeting at CHARTERHALL on 28th June. Combined car and motor cycle.

There was plenty to do sports-wise. These adverts are from What's On guides for 1958-59. Also featured are horse racing, rugby football, gliding, ice skating, cricket and much else.

All I Have to do is Dream

Everly Brothers, 1958

Out to work

My first proper job was with the London and Newcastle Tea Company on St James Street. I was the office junior and used to address the envelopes and type little things. We had a supervisor, three older girls and another junior. We were allowed to do some invoices using carbon paper, but the supervisor was very fussy about it – she was always reminding us to put the carbon back in the box as it had to be used again.

I also used the franking machine. We had branches all over the North East and sent stuff out every night. We had to take turns to do the post, put it through the franking machine and record the cost of each frank in a book. You had to count the pennies and halfpennies to make sure that it balanced before you took the packages to the post office in Gallowgate. The next morning you had to check it all again.

One morning, after checking the book twice the previous night, it was wrong by a halfpenny. My friend said, 'Just put down another letter and it'll be right'. So I did that and put the book away. Then the supervisor asked 'did you balance the book?' I said 'Yes'. She said

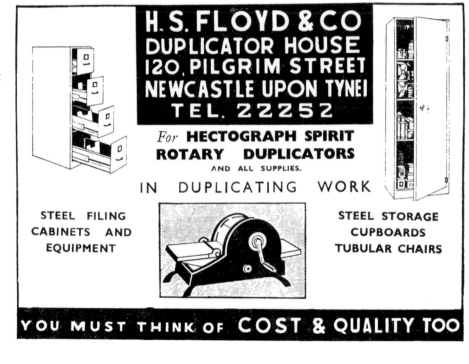

'Is it correct?' I said 'Yes'. She said 'It can't possibly be correct, because after you'd gone last night I sent a letter for Mr Reed, and I didn't write it in the book.' She was testing my honesty. And the other girl just sat there and never said a word. I was 15. I just thought 'Well that's lesson number one kid, and you've learned it.' There were some awful bosses. I was near to tears. They made out I was a liar.

I soon got another job. A neighbour said the Co-op on Blandford Street was a good place to work. So I wrote an application and got an interview. My mother came with me. I had to do tests in maths and English. I got an extra 11 shillings a week, and half day off on Saturday.

I used to wear pencil slim skirts and flat shoes and twin sets. I had a Co-op card and could get discount in the drapery department. As typists we used to work for a bonus of 4s a week. So many people worked for the Co-op that when I came out of the building at night time it was like a football match.

Norah Coombes

Climbing the career ladder

I started work in 1951 immediately after my 15th birthday. My first job was with John B. Bowes, a printing firm at the end of Low Friar Street. I was the office junior and it was my job to run errands, one of which, of course, was to make the tea and go around to the café on Westgate Road for toasted teacakes for everyone.

The building was very old and it was overrun with mice. I wasn't scared of them so the other girls used to wait until I arrived to open up the office and disperse the mice before they would enter. Across the road from our office was a former public house, the Fountain, where we kept all the old files, and again it was my job to go over and open up to retrieve old documents. As soon as I opened the door I was greeted by rodents, but this time they were rats! Fortunately they scarpered rapidly.

My typing skills improved but my shorthand did not as I got no experience. There were no photocopiers in those days so if you needed to make extra copies, you had to use carbon paper and very flimsy paper. Everything was very formal, anyone senior to me was given their full title and there was no chit-chat amongst the girls. We worked a five-and-a-half day week, finishing at 1pm on a Saturday, for a weekly wage of £1 15s.

My next job was at a firm called Semtex Ltd, a subsidiary of The Dunlop Rubber Company, who supplied and laid very fine floor coverings on ships and in hotels and public houses. Nothing at all to do with explosives! This company was in Jesmond, quite near to the Royal Grammar School. I was now a shorthand typist and answered the telephone too! I didn't work on Saturday mornings and got £2 10s per week.

After this, I moved to Robert Stephenson and Hawthorns, at the corner of Forth Street and Forth Banks, where steam locomotives were built and shipped all over the world. I was now a more senior shorthand typist working for the General Manager. Across the road from my office was The Empire Bacon Company and almost every other day there were huge lorries carrying squealing pigs going to slaughter. Sometimes the men had difficulties with one or two pigs who were very anxious to escape becoming bacon. I couldn't eat bacon for quite a while afterwards. To get to Forth Banks from Neville Street, I would come down a pathway called 'The Cut', which apparently belonged to British Rail, and on one day a year I had to pay a penny for the privilege of using it.

Changing jobs in those days was very easy, but in 1959, when the factory was no longer producing steam locomotives because of the more modern diesel-electric engines, I decided it was time to look for something different and so

joined the WRAC where I served for three years as a shorthand typist working initially in Whitehall before being posted out to Cyprus.

Anon

Counting the pennies

At the beginning of the decade I had already worked for two years as an apprentice accountant and had another three years ahead of me. Work involved a five-and-a-half day week at a local firm of accountants on Sandyford Road, as well as studying at home (around 15 hours a week) by way of a correspondence course. This was the normal route for most accounting students at that time. Saturday morning work was usual for the majority of office employees. With regard to annual holiday, the most you could hope for was one week. Virtually all my home study took place in the bathroom (no, not in the bath) where quietness and warmth were guaranteed.

Having successfully passed the intermediate exam in 1950 (which meant spending two or three days in Leeds) I was pleased to receive a pay increase which saw my weekly income rise from five shillings to £3 before deductions for tax and National Insurance.

It was possible to park vehicles near the office in those days of no yellow lines, though some clients arrived by tram (still running along Sandyford Road in the early 1950s) or on foot, but on one occasion, to my surprise, an antique dealer turned up with his papers on horseback and tethered the horse to the nearest lamp post.

Much of the work of trainee accountants was to visit clients' premises to inspect the books with a view to preparing annual accounts for the business. On one of these visits to a small firm in the Ouseburn Valley, I innocently inquired as to the whereabouts of the toilet. The rather stern looking office manager standing at his high Dickensian desk replied 'The Ouseburn is just around the corner lad and for something more involved try the garage up the road'. Even in central Newcastle it was not uncommon for male office

195

workers to have to use public toilets or nearby pubs. Women sometimes seemed to be better provided for.

Our office was an all-male environment with a lack of facilities for women. A much older man ruled the general office and if he thought you were engaging in idle chatter, he would quickly ask if there was a particular problem. All staff had to complete daily time sheets so that clients could be charged the correct amount for the hours spent on a job. In an age of austerity the issue of stationery was under strict control and we were encouraged to re-use scrap paper and old envelopes for draft letters and workings out. No calculators were available although a cumbersome adding machine did exist. Carbon paper (which could be messy) was used to make duplicate copies. All incoming mail was date stamped and recorded manually, and outgoing mail had to be recorded in a postage book which then had to be balanced with the number of stamps in hand.

However, some things were to change with the departure of the chief clerk for pastures new. Our boss decided to employ his first female member of staff. This may have been an effect of National Service where 18-year-olds were conscripted into the armed forces for two years. Our new staff member was a war widow and much older than any of us but she was an efficient secretary and typist. Most importantly she brought in some fundamental changes such as the introduction of tea breaks in the morning and the afternoon. Later, biscuits became part of the routine!

Nevertheless our lady secretary did cause some problems, one of these being feeding the birds on our wide Victorian window sill, we even had the occasional bird flying round the office. Eventually the neighbours complained about the mess and it had to stop.

At another time she befriended a stray cat and fed it in the general office. This went on for a few weeks until it all ended in disaster for her (and amusement for the rest of us) owing to the unexpected footsteps of the senior partner as he approached the office. Suddenly the cat and saucer were hurriedly deposited into a deep drawer of her desk and out of sight (but not out of hearing). She held onto her job, but I don't recall further cats in the office.

In 1954, shortly after this incident and having passed my final exams, it was my turn to do National Service, having been deferred for five years.

Alan Morgan

Working for Parsons

Before the days of photocopiers or computer aided design, if you wanted to copy a plan of anything from a machine to a mine, you had make a tracing of it onto fine linen cloth that had been coated to make it smooth and transparent. These tracings were put onto a huge machine that made prints.

I was a tracer, and in the early 1950s I was working for Parsons in Heaton, tracing plans for turbines and other machinery. Tracing was a difficult art to master. If you got the tracing cloth wet, the special coating started to dissolve and you were left with a mess of damp linen. Everything had to be 100 per cent accurate and as you used Indian ink, you couldn't correct mistakes but had to start again from scratch. This didn't make you popular. During the war I'd served an apprenticeship in tracing at Clarke Chapman in Gateshead, so by 1950 I was quite experienced. This meant I could spot mistakes in the original plans that I was copying – If that happened I'd ask one of the draughtsmen to correct it.

Parsons employed a lot of tracers, but most of them worked in the tracing office in another building. In my drawing office there were 23 draughtsmen and engineers, all male, two typists (female, of course), who had their own little office, and me. Working in a male-dominated environment was fine. They could

A splitter vessel en route from Parsons in Heaton to Shellhaven via Scrogg Road, Walker, 1956.

make suggestive comments, but I'd just give them a look of distain and they'd stop very quickly.

I was married with a toddler, but there was never any question of me having to give up work as other married women did – the country was relying on the engineering industry to get it back on its feet after the war and my skills were in demand. However it was made very clear to me that I couldn't use my family as an excuse for lateness or absence.

As part of war reparations, the Allies decided that German engineers should share their knowledge. This meant that several German engineers worked in our office. It was only a few years since the war had ended, and you might have expected resentments to surface on both sides, but actually everyone worked very well together. The Germans were far in advance of us in many ways, which meant that my work got a lot more complicated.

Some of the cleverest engineers were working on an 'unofficial' project to build a sports car from 'leftover' bits and pieces. They often asked me to trace plans for them in my 'spare' time. I saw the car once when they first trialled it, but after that they kept modifying it so I don't think it was ever completed.

Agnes Chilton

The draughtsman

I started at Vickers Armstrong in 1955 and worked in the VSG drawing office, making drawings for hydraulic pumps and motors.

One day, just before Christmas, one of my colleagues suggested that I should take a look in the ADO (Armament Drawing Office). I was absolutely astonished by what I saw. All the benches in the place were covered by structures, mainly of card and paper. There were ingenious working models, tableaux, pictures and all sorts of things, including a ghost train, which crashed through cardboard swing doors, into a long tunnel and round again. On its way the train would knock against trip levers that caused little doors to open and expose skeletons and the like.

A model of Vickers main entrance stood on one bench and across a gangway was a model of the Moulder's Arms (a pub on the other side of Scotswood Road). Aerial ropes connected the two, with little cars shunting back and forth continually.

In 1957, the year of the Sputnik, besides the usual stuff there were about 50 of these satellites hanging from the ceiling. Part of this enthusiasm for Russian space travel was due to the socialist leanings of most of the staff.

The displays were all scrapped and thrown away between Christmas and New Year, and all was earnest normality until late November when it started again. In the VSG, by contrast, there was never so much as a robin. One year the ADO sent us a cardboard coffin labelled 'the spirit of Christmas'.

The canteen in which we draughtsmen ate was set with little tables with places for four. One corner of the room was partitioned off with metal framing and frosted glass. The tables had cloths, water jugs and glasses. This was where the section leaders and senior clerks ate. I believe there were at least three other canteens catering for successively higher seniorities of staff, culminating in the Directors' Mess, which had its own kitchen and serving staff. This was in stark contrast to the shopfloor workers' canteen, which was inconveniently situated on the other side of Scotswood Road and furnished with long, bare trestle tables and forms.

Vickers provided a free lending library that contained many thousands of books. Each book that was lent out was given a paper cover at the issue desk. This was very sensible considering the oily hands of the workers. What was odd was that the jackets had been made for extremely intellectual books, so you could see a dirty-handed labourer

Top, the drawing office at Vickers around 1950.
Right, some serious engineering at Vickers at the end of the 1950s.

carrying away a book that purported to be 'Essays on Neo Platonism', but was actually 'Gunsmoke at the Lazy Y' by Zane Grey!

Eric Shields (extract from 'Voices from Vickers', Tyne Bridge Publishing, 2001)

The challenge of teaching

In September 1951 I started my teaching career at Cambridge Street Infants' School. The school was a large Victorian building on Rye Hill with the infants on the ground floor, juniors on the first floor and secondary pupils on the second – all topped off by a playground on the roof.

The interior of the infants' school had a long dark corridor, with the staff room near the entrance, leading to the Head Mistress's room at the other end. The classrooms were all in a line along one side of the corridor with a multi-purpose hall on the other – it was used for assemblies, physical education, music and dinners.

A lot of the staff had been there for many years and loved the school in spite of all its problems.

The classrooms had high windows (opened by a long pole with a hook on the end) that the children could not see through. The teacher's desk was high with a high stool for the teacher to perch upon! Children's desks for two were being replaced by bright little tables, also for two, and the teacher was able to walk about to help the children.

In my first class I taught 47 five year olds for which I received £18 a month. I was thrilled after a year or two when this rose to £20.

As for the children, they were fascinating – friendly, open scruffy, non-academic, very street-wise (even the very young

Terry Quinn

The First Eleven. Denton Road School junior champions, 1955.

Cambridge Street School with its rooftop playground in the mid-1960s.

ones) but at the same time mischievous and loveable. As I came from Yorkshire I could not always understand them as their Geordie accents were very pronounced. On a few occasions when I took a child home I was amazed at the conditions in which they lived. The school was surrounded by lovely old Victorian houses but each one was occupied by several families – sometimes sharing one toilet and a stand pipe in the back yard. The vast majority of the children were on free meals and we suspected that that was their only meal of the day. At Christmas time schools in the other suburbs sent their little used toys for our children.

Each child had an 'attendance slip', which was a sheet of paper showing the school terms with a space for each day that had to be marked when a child was absent. On the reverse the teacher entered the reason for absence – M for measles, C for chicken pox and significantly N.B. for 'No Books'! Although I don't recall having to use the latter mark, I am aware that some of my colleagues did.

The children of course were subject to conditions that thankfully are not so prevalent these days – fleas, scabies and impetigo. Unfortunately these conditions sometimes transferred themselves to the staff – we just had to get over it!

At the time I was living in a comfortable flat in Jesmond, travelling to school by trolley bus to the Central Station and walking over what the children called 'the buildings' although there were no buildings as they had been bombed during the war and at that stage not re-built. The contrast between home and school was quite dramatic though I don't think I appreciated it at the time.

Because the children had so little, anything you gave them or did for them was appreciated by both the children and their parents. All in all it was an experience I would not have missed. Cambridge Street School is no longer there, although it did for a time become part of Newcastle College. I have happy memories of my time there and I hope that some of the youngsters remember their school days with pleasure.

Margaret Carter

If you want to know the time …

I first joined the Police Force in 1947 as a 16-year-old police cadet and was a cadet until I was 18 when I did two years' National Service in the RAF. During National Service I was a member of the RAF police. In 1951, at the age of 20, I re-joined Newcastle City Police as a police constable. I had a short chat with the Chief Constable and was accepted immediately because of my previous experience. In those days the minimum height for a police officer was 5ft 10 ins. During the first two years of service, police officers were on probation, and their services could be dispensed with without notice.

Eric Green

Eric's collar badge.

We operated a three shift system: 6am-2pm, 2pm-10pm and 10pm-6am. Discipline was exacting and called for rigid time keeping at the start and end of the shift, out on the beat and for refreshment periods. If you were as little as two or three minutes late it would mean a visit to the Superintendant who could order you to carry out extra hours at the end of your shift

If you were based in the centre of the city, you went to Pilgrim Street for your break. You were timed arriving and leaving. If there was an emergency during break, you had to go and deal with it and were not allowed to finish your break later.

When I joined the force, we worked eight-hour shifts, and refreshments were taken in wooden police boxes strategically placed across the city (see photo of the Bigg Market, page 91). Inside the boxes, there was a wooden bench, a telephone and a stool. Sometimes, they had a one bar electric fire. They had no facilities for refreshments or even making a drink. Hot drinks were scrounged from somewhere on the beat.

I remember one police box in Jesmond that had no electricity, no heating, and you had to take your own candle if you wanted to read a paper or do any paperwork. You had no option but to sit there, even in the middle of a snowy

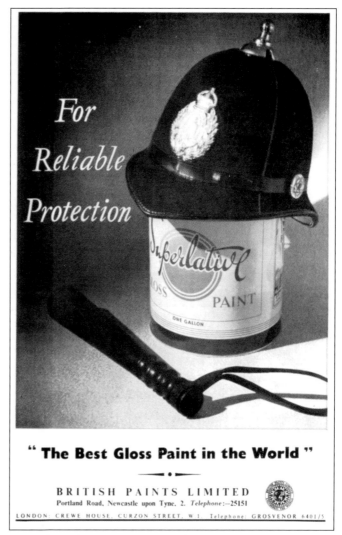

An advert from Newcastle Official Guide, 1956.

winter. We had a half-hour refreshment break with an additional quarter of an hour taken at another time during the shift.

There was no access to toilets when on the beat, and no toilet facilities in the police boxes. We had to make our own arrangements!

Police boxes were also used for taking and giving messages, writing reports, and for retaining prisoners before they could be taken to Pilgrim Street Police Station. The boxes had Yale locks that were often faulty, so it could be difficult to retain prisoners until the police van could collect them. Each division had a police van and a motor car.

If you needed assistance you had to go to nearest telephone box. We all had a whistle to blow to attract the attention of other officers but it depended on the time of day as to whether anyone responded.

A PC's uniform included a closed neck tunic with high neck and a half belt, made from heavy blue serge. It was worn with a collarless blue shirt. In winter you wore a heavy blue serge overcoat and cape. You couldn't just wear the cape on its own, you always had to wear the overcoat underneath it. You had a helmet with chin strap, white gloves in summer and black gloves in winter and on night duty. In summer, the uniform was hot and uncomfortable. In the rain, it became sodden and even heavier.

CRIMINAL INVESTIGATION DEPARTMENT, NEWCASTLE UPON TYNE CITY POLICE.

DINNER
AND
SMOKING CONCERT

at the

LIBERAL CLUB, PILGRIM STREET,
Newcastle upon Tyne,

on

Friday, January 25th, 1957.

Dinner at 7-30 p.m. prompt.

Chairman :
ROBT. W. DAVISON, Det./Supt.

A CID dinner and concert, 1957. Smoking was permitted (but not compulsory!) during the performance. Eric joined the CID in 1956.

You had to provide your own boots, torch batteries and bulb, although there was a boot and lamp allowance to cover the cost. A PC's equipment consisted of a truncheon, handcuffs, torch, whistle and notebook.

On point duty you wore white gloves and long waterproof white coat.

In Newcastle City Police Force there was a handful of female police officers: one Inspector, one Sergeant and five or six WPCs. They had to be at least 5ft 4ins tall (without boots). They assisted in matters relating to women and children. One of their duties involved giving vouchers to parents who couldn't afford to buy school shoes for their children. Only one female police officer was on duty at night, normally based at Pilgrim Street. One of their nightly duties was to check all female public toilets in the city, accompanied by a male PC. They were looking out for prostitutes and homeless people.

At first my wife and I had a flat in Wallsend. On Sunday mornings there was no transport if you were on early shift so I had to walk into Newcastle and then go straight onto the beat.

I went onto the police housing list when got married. Police houses were rent-free. In 1958 we moved into a brand new police house in Provost Gardens, Benwell. It was a three-bedroom house with indoor plumbing and a garden and a complete contrast to our one-bedroom flat with an outside toilet and a tin bath. Provost Gardens was a cul-de-sac of eight police houses, and was occupied by families with young children. It was a very close knit community.

One day the circus, including a herd of performing elephants, arrived at the Central Railway Station Goods Yard. As a junior constable, I was told to walk at the rear of the elephants and to follow the procession from the Central Station to the Town Moor. Imagine walking through the streets of Newcastle on a busy Sunday morning, avoiding piles of elephant poo!

Eric Green, PC352, retired Inspector Northumbria Police

Police telephone near West Jesmond School, 1956.

When I joined the Newcastle City Police in 1954 I quickly found that the public followed the advice of the 1880s music hall song and often asked the policeman – polis – copper – bobby – old bill – whatever name you choose, for the correct time, notwithstanding that we were not issued with watches. What the Newcastle Watch Committee did provide was one of the smartest police uniforms in the country. Peak caps, dark fine serge tunics, with blue shirts, black ties and white cotton gloves for day wear. At night we used closed neck tunics, helmets with the badge plates blacked out and black wool gloves. The city fathers understood the need to protect its police against the weather with greatcoats, raincoats and capes. The sergeants and inspectors worked hard to keep the standards up.

Today's drug culture and the use of knives and guns were not the same then, and the weight of road traffic was much less. But the range of theft, breaking and entering and so forth remained the same problem in the 1950s as it had been since 1836 when the first policemen began patrolling the streets of the Borough of Newcastle upon Tyne.

Police recruit training for the North East took place at Newby Wiske near Northallerton. That lasted for three months, followed by a long period of familiarisation where recruits spent a shift with an experienced constable on each foot beat in the whole of the city and each department such as CID and Traffic. Recruits were then posted to a police division and let loose on the streets, in my case 'B' Newcastle West Division. The city of Newcastle was smaller then, 'B' filled the space between the river and Fawdon in the north and Westgate to Denton Square in the west.

No cars or radios for the bobbies on the beat, of course. There was one divisional car (a Wolseley) and one general purpose van. But there was a strategy for the foot patrols that made the best possible use of manpower. The West Division was divided into 18 foot beats and spread out on the boundaries of each of the beats were at least three police boxes shared by the officers on adjoining beats. The police box was the inspiration for the Tardis in *Doctor Who*, but the inside of a Newcastle police box could not be described as high tech. There was a telephone connected to the DHQ at Westgate Road opposite the General Hospital for

Barry Redfern

Barry Redfern on Pilgrim Street. He was snapped by a local newsagent trying out a new camera.

police and public emergency use, and a light on top of the box could be flashed to call the beat officer. Inside was simply a tall stool and a flat surface on which to write reports.

There were three shifts starting at 6am, 2pm and 10pm and a system for the officer to start duty, not at the police box, but at a nominated point somewhere on his beat and to finish duty at a different nominated point. These changed daily. So, as one officer started duty at one point, another officer was ending duty at a different location. At shift change time this was occurring all across the city, effectively doubling the police presence on the streets for a spell. A constable would often find a sergeant or inspector waiting at the start or finish point so failure to attend had to be followed by a very good explanation.

The only contact with DHQ was by telephone once per hour (never from the same police box) and supervision visits by the inspectors and sergeants. It trained policemen to become resourceful and self-reliant. Walking for the full shift each day induced a good level of physical fitness.

Senior officers laid heavy stress on the protection of property. The beat patrols were responsible for ensuring that all lock-up premises, such as public houses, had been properly secured, and checking them throughout the night.

In the 1950s there was a pub on just about every corner on Scotswood Road. In the early hours one morning, my colleague Don and I spotted intruders in one of these pubs. The front was secure. Don went one way round the back and I the other. Then I heard shouts and found Don struggling with one of the burglars, who was trying desperately to escape. It was as much as we could do to hold the prisoner, but then a second burglar came out of the pub yard. He was less trouble, but trying to move these prisoners to the police box about 400 or 500 yards away was quite a problem. There was a lot of noise, of course, and a woman awakened by the racket came to the back door of a house behind the pub and asked if we were OK. She was heaven-sent and I asked her to run along to the police box at the foot of Gloucester Street and telephone for assistance. Help arrived quickly, the prisoners knew the game was up and went along quietly. A third member of this gang was arrested within the hour and in due time all three were sent to prison. What a difference modern technology would have made!

Policing Scotswood Road on foot meant that we had personal contact with the residents every hour of the day so there was a good community spirit despite the falling standards of old housing. One of our regular

The police box on Gloucester Street.

Jimmy Forsyth photographed the length of Scotswood Road in 1956, before much of it was demolished. Here is the Gladstone Hotel on the corner of Clumber Street, and further along are Dodds the butcher and Hay the chemist (known locally as Dr Hay).

commitments, morning and evening, was to see the men and women safely in and out of work at the Armstrong factories. All of the beat officers along there learned how King Canute must have felt if he really did try to stem the flow of the tides. As the 'go-home' hooter sounded, hundreds of workers poured out of the gates. There was a lot of good natured banter as we tried to organise the traffic safely but come what may they would be across the road for their buses. It was an exciting daily challenge to combine pedestrian safety with traffic movement, fortunately it didn't take long.

School crossing patrols had not yet been developed and the police got more and more requests to provide safe crossing for children going to school. The innocent interest of young children in the police was a sheer delight; there were lots of cheerful shouts of 'Thank you' as they crossed the road and it was a good way of building up trust. When the demolition of houses began in the Fifties, one of the continuing problems was keeping children out of dangerous half-demolished properties as they were a magnet for the young people. For months on end there was a smell of plaster dust hanging in the air.

Another view of Scotswood Road by Jimmy Forsyth. The Royal Oak was at the corner of Ivy Street and Scotswood Road.

As policemen we saw the disastrous effects of heavy drinking all too clearly. All those pubs on Scotswood Road had their customers. On weekend nights we would double up at pub closing time to provide a visible deterrent to drunken violence. We saw the aftermath of domestic violence and the poverty caused by family income being wasted on alcohol. It was sad to witness that.

The other thing I remember is the pleasure of observing the city settling down for the night, the sunset, the roads and the pavements slowly clearing of traffic and people, and then the household lights going out. Then the signs of the city awakening and starting up again for a new day; the milkmen, the postmen off to work, the delivery of newspapers and the newsagents opening up, the early buses, street cleaners and the sun rising.

Barry Redfern, retired Chief Superintendent, Northumbria Police

I worked at Terry's [hairdressers] on the Coast Road in 1958 or 1959. The girls from the Wills factory would come in for perms. As far as fashion went, the place was out of the ark! Then I went to Mortimers on Claremont Road which was another world. Customers would arrive in Rolls Royces.

Pauline Luke

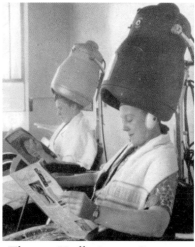

Thomas Hedley's tests Drene shampoo at City Road, 1953.

My first job was in Murton's but I liked going out on a Saturday afternoon with my friends. I heard you got a Saturday half day at Fenwick's, so I got a job there.

Fenwick's was very snobby; you weren't allowed to speak to anyone that came in. We had to wear a green uniform and they docked five shillings out of your wages to cover the cost. I started in millinery – there were two sections, one at the front door and one at the back. Miss Graham was our buyer and Miss Trainer the under buyer. There were three juniors. We had to dust the stands and put the hats on display. Customers could take hats home on approval on a Friday night. There was one woman who'd take three hats and bring them back on a Monday – we knew she'd worn them over the weekend. We used to buy in stock and then sew in the Fenwick's label in by hand. Mr Fenwick would come and walk round the whole shop. The young Fenwick boys worked in all the departments to get experience.

Carol Wilson

210

In 1953 when I reached 15 and was about to leave school, I saw the careers officer to discuss jobs. I decided to apply for a vacancy in the Stylo Shoe Shop in Clayton Street. The job was okay, but I wasn't allowed to do much at first. My mam suggested I try something else and immediately I was offered a job at Parrish's on Shields Road. This was great as it was only a walk away from home with no bus fares to pay. Parrish's was a big department store that sold everything and even had a food department.

Clayton Street, Stylo on the left, 1958.

I started on the boys' department. Before I could serve I had to know all about the stock, materials and sizes. I had to be able to judge the right size for any boy aged five or more. Sometimes Mr Geoffrey Parrish, who was very hands-on in the store, came to talk about the stock. My immediate boss was Mr Wade, a buyer who was in charge of the menswear department, selling suits, trousers and overalls for work.

Our uniform was black but later on we had green suits, which we paid for out of our wages.

People used to pay by Provident Orders (see page 152). They would take them to the Bureau and get them changed for tokens you could only use at Parrish's. When a customer paid for their purchase, I put the money into a container that was whisked away by a tube to the cashier's office. The cashiers would send the change back in a similar container.

At Christmas we would often be asked to help on the food department, as our department was quiet at that time of year.

We used to work until 4.30pm with a half day on Wednesdays finishing at 1pm. There was once a strike by the staff, as we wanted the hours to stay as they were but management wanted to change them.

Compared with today's opening hours, I certainly know what I'd prefer!

While at Parrish's, I went to night classes at Middle Street School to learn shorthand and typing and English. Most people did night classes to better themselves, but I was quite happy being a shop assistant. I stayed at Parrish's until I got married; after that I spent about a year at Farnon's, learning how to cut and match curtains!

Margaret Bingham (née Molly Johnson)

Working for the GPO

I worked for the GPO in Newcastle from 1943 to 1954. In the 1950s before automation, sorting letters and parcels was done by hand. I was a sorting clerk at the Orchard Street office and remember how we had to stand for an entire eight-hour shift sorting letters into the appropriate pigeon holes. We were encouraged to work fast and if we finished our allocation we were directed to another set of pigeon holes. There was no escape. The minutes ticked away on a railway station sized clock and we worked until the very last minute when the overseer would call out, 'Break away lads!' There were no first and second class postage rates 60

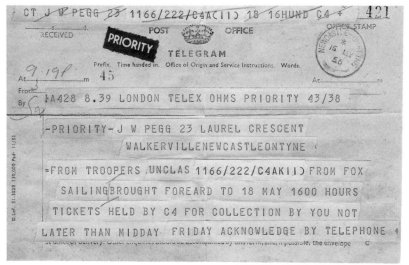

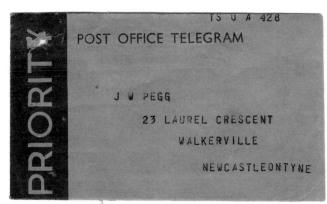

This urgent telegram was sent to me by the War Office giving instructions and calling for confirmation of receipt by telephone. It was sent at 8.39pm in London and received at 9.19 in Newcastle date stamped 18th May 1956. It is marked priority because it is OHMS (On Her Majesty's Service) and very urgent. Joe Pegg

212

years ago; the public placed their confidence in the post office system to get the mail there as fast as possible, which is what we all aimed to achieve, working day and night to do so.

The Post Office together with Post Office Telephones was the communications hub of the city. Telephone and telegrams were, in the early 1950s, the fastest means of communication. Private telephones were much less common then, so if you wanted to ring someone you had to find a telephone box. If you were lucky enough to find one that had not been vandalized, or was not out of order, or did not have a queue waiting outside because the person using the box was making a lengthy call and kept putting coins in the box, you entered the telephone box where you could make your call in absolute privacy. First you needed the correct coins. You put the coins in the box and dialled the number. If the person called answered you pressed Button A to make the connection. If not you pressed Button B to get your money back. If your call overran the time for which you had paid, you were cut off in mid sentence, so calls were of necessity short and sweet!

Telegrams were sent from a post office, where you told the clerk what you wanted to say and he told you how much it would cost. As the art of costing a telegram was a mystery to all, heated discussions often ensued between customer and clerk. The wording was written on an official telegram form and sent off to the Head Post Office in a container by an underground pneumatic tube. It arrived in the Instrument Room, where rows and rows of young women, sitting at teleprinters, were sending and receiving telegrams from other towns and cities. From here it was sent by teleprinter land line to its destination and on arrival it was delivered on an official form in a distinctive yellow envelope by messenger boy into the hands of the recipient. All of this took only a matter of a few hours.

Within the confined area of the town there were five headquarters branch offices located at Blackett Street, Gallowgate, Barras Bridge, Neville Street and Quayside. They are long gone.

Joe Pegg

More jobs for the girls

1957 was not a good year for my family. My elder sister developed yellow jaundice and died at the age of just 19. A month later my father went into hospital for a minor operation and suffered two heart attacks on the operating table: he survived, but was judged to be permanently unfit for work. It was decided that I must leave school immediately, for my large family needed whatever I could earn.

I was due to take 'O' Levels, but instead left school and began work as a junior clerk at the College of Commerce in College Street, where I earned the princely sum of £2 15s per week, paid monthly, for a five-and-a-half-day week, 8.45 until 5.15 each day and 8.45 until 12.15 on Saturdays.

My job involved managing the small switchboard – I never did quite get the hang of that – and running off loads of notes for the lecturers on the inky Gestetner copier in a tiny annexe at the other end of the building. I also had to make sure we had enough stamps for the daily post – a worry solved when the franking machine arrived.

On Mondays my first task was to purchase a week's supply of mixed biscuits for the morning coffee breaks. This involved some subterfuge for the office manager, Miss Rule, the two secretaries, Miss Brown and Miss Harrison, and the senior clerk, Miss Douglas insisted that I shop at Fenwick's. Unfortunately, there was never quite enough in the coffee break funds to provide a satisfactory range within the price constraints, so I sneakily bought the biscuits from the large Woolworths' on Northumberland Street and carried them back in a Fenwick's carrier bag kept just for the task.

Notice the formality of the titles. We were always referred to as 'Miss' or 'Mrs': a custom that began to change slowly over the next couple of years. Miss Harrison and Miss Brown were in their mid and late thirties and had resigned themselves to spinsterhood. They were good friends and were the first women I knew to take package summer holidays abroad, which was considered very adventurous at the time.

A year later I left the College of Commerce and transferred to the Newcastle School Health Service. I loved the work, which took me all over the city delivering vaccines and keeping clinical records, but my mother loathed my new job. She was desperately afraid that I'd bring home something nasty and pass it on to my youngest brother and sister.

From my point of view, I had a major financial problem for the City Medical Service insisted that its lowly clerks' expenses were paid retrospectively each month and at the lowest journey rate, despite the fact that the clinic timetables necessitated a swift transfer between each site. I was, in fact, subsidising the School Health Service. Often, at the end of the month, my pockets were empty and I had no choice but to spend my hungry lunch hour walking from Benwell to Heaton via the City Road headquarters from which I collected the vacuum flasks for each vaccination session.

Finding work was never a problem, although wages for young people were low and, once past 18, we had National Insurance deducted from our salaries even though they were too small to be taxable.

Reluctantly, I left Local Government and went to work briefly for British Railways at the very grubby Central Station, which still had steam trains. Then I moved on to Thomas Hedley who manufactured soap powders and shampoos at their factory in City Road, close to the new Tyne Tees Television studio. At that time, Hedley's were zealously promoting Camay soap, containing a perfume that cost 'Nine guineas per ounce' – a price that the British public found ridiculously unbelievable. I was employed at the Buying Office in Collingwood Street, a thoroughfare consisting mainly of elegant banks and insurance companies, just as Grey Street was the address of the various embassies, consulates and law firms.

The concept of being 'a teenager' had not quite established itself in the north east, despite the odd few 'teddy boys' seen around the city in their draped jackets, drainpipe trousers and crepe-soled shoes. Whilst young women dreamed of boy friends with their own vehicle, young men dreamed of owning a car. Most, however, were happy to drive a

Procter & Gamble

NEWCASTLE (*Below*) Every week more than a dozen Hedley people dance in front of the television cameras in the Tyne-Tees studios. They are the coffee-bar 'customers' at The Golden Disc — an amateur talent show. Among the habitués of this highly public café, some of whom we photographed, are Ken Atkinson (*Industrial Engineering*), Elaine Besford (*Public Relations Department*), Pat Douglas (*Manufacturing Headquarters*), Sheila Fairs (*Engineering Division*), Pat Frazer (*Industrial Engineering*), Dorothy Gall (*Hospital Sister*) and her husband. Maureen Grant (*Manufacturing Headquarters*) and her husband. Norma Gray (*Industrial Engineering*), Miriam Jones (*Industrial Relations*) and her husband. Norman McGregor (*Industrial Engineering*) and Mrs McGregor. Joy Nichol (*Plant Engineer's Office*), David Rixon (*Safety and Training Manager, Newcastle Factory*) and Mrs Rixon. Ted Ward (*Works Administration Department*), Pauline Wilkinson (*Buying Department*) and Fred Wind (*Technical Service and Packaging Department*).

A page from the Thomas Hedley staff magazine, Moonbeams, April 1959.

motorbike or a Lambretta scooter until they achieved their dream vehicle. In any case, at eighteen, unless they were apprentices, in which case it was delayed until they were 21, they were whisked away to do National Service in the army, navy or air-force.

In the North East, some girls still expected to give up work once they were married. Others, such as Post Office telephonists, were obliged to resign on marriage. That is not to say that married women did not work – they did indeed work but were often apologetic about their need to do so!

Maureen Brook

Book keeping?

The City's Central Library played an important part in Newcastle's life during the 1950s. It was busy and well-used. At that time it encompassed a section of the old city walls and that part of the building was known to the library staff as 'the half circle'. On the ground floor occupying that particular area was the library's fiction collection.

The library faced on to New Bridge Street. A small but elegant flight of steps led from street level to doors opening into a spacious hall, from which a broad staircase rose to a half landing. A large stained glass window there filtered coloured light over the whole hall. Stairs from the half landing led from the left and right to reach the first floor and the Reference Library. To the right of this was the Bewick Room where glass cases displayed examples of the engravings and wood blocks that the famous illustrator, Thomas Bewick used in his work. Beyond this to the right was the first floor's section of the 'half-circle'. This was used as a storage space for the Reference Library.

There was a door beside the Bewick Room, used by the staff climbing up to the second floor and to the staff rooms. There were two staff rooms – one for ladies only and the other one for all members of staff. There were facilities for making tea and coffee, lockers for personal belongings, and even an oven I think. On a sunny day staff could climb out of the window and disport themselves on the sun-drenched ledges on the roof. It was quite a journey from the ground floor and staff taking their precious 15 minute break had to allow time for the journey up aloft and the return journey.

The other 'reference' library was the Business and Technical Library, which was on one side of the ground floor. It was quite important locally. The Lending Library was opposite, on the left. It was very well used. There were experiments in new ways of issuing and returning books and queues would quite often build up.

The cellar regions were reached from the rear of the hall to the left. These warm dark recesses were presided over by janitors, the chief of whom was Mr Harry Tupman. With a name like 'Tupman' and a staff of librarians with literary tastes, Mr Tupman soon became known as 'Tracey' after the character in Charles Dickens's *Pickwick*

Local Studies staff demonstrate their head for heights, around 1949.

Papers. Library janitors are traditionally important members of staff and Mr Tupman would field one of the 'characters' from the Reference Library staff who sometimes got a little tipsy on his evenings off and would return to work still in that state. There would have been trouble had he been seen by senior members of staff so 'Tracey' would take him down to the cellars to sober up.

The library was a favourite refuge for the down and outs who used to seek shelter at night in the Salvation Army Palace, but who were sent out in the morning. The library was a nice warm place and there were newspapers to read. They were not

Staff on the steps of the junior library.

really welcome but often stayed none the less. There was one who haunted the Music Section in the Lending Library. He was musical and would give you a short rendering of *Caro mio ben*. He was unfortunately what one librarian called an 'olfactory nuisance' and was very smelly. He often managed to button-hole borrowers who came into the Music Section and tell them his story.

The library had a cat. It was acquired no doubt because of mice in that warm place – the cellar. He was on the library pay-roll. He was all white but when a member of staff tried to make a friend and pet of him, he was completely unresponsive. So she christened him 'Wooden'. During a long holiday weekend another member of staff took him home with her. He sat quite happily on her lap during the bus ride to her home and back. White cats, I learned later, are quite often deaf, which might have explained poor Wooden's behaviour.

Margaret Oates

Christmas party, Central Library, 1950s.

Newcastle City Libraries started to operate their first mobile library van on 1 November, 1950. It was a boon to elderly people living on outlying estates with no library nearby.

The 1950s was an exciting time for the library service. It was the decade in which the British National Bibliography was set up and local cataloguing became less important. Inter-library loans acquired a teleprinter, which seemed quite a marvel. Change was in the air!

Margaret Oates (née Lawson)

My first job, in 1954, was working for the Northumberland Territorial and Auxiliary Armed Forces in Sandyford Road, (pictured right) where everyone was called Miss, Mrs, Mr, Captain, Major or Brigadier; no Christian names except among the junior staff. I was paid £3 a week. The offices were upstairs and the drill hall was downstairs; we drew lots to go down there and face the licentious remarks of the chap who doled out the various things, 'officers for the use of'. We wore dresses or skirts and blouses at work – wearing trousers would never have been even considered – and pastel coloured twinsets bought in a small shop in a street off Northumberland Street. My favourite occupation at work was being allowed to operate the switchboard: there's power in being able to say to someone rather important: 'Hold the line, please, Major,' or 'I'm putting you through now, sir.'

Jane Jantet

My dad was reading the *Evening Chronicle* and drew my attention to a notice inviting girls over 17 years old to volunteer for Queen Alexandra's Royal Army Nursing Corps in the Territorial Army. I was interested and decided to go to Fenham Militia Camp the following night after work. There I was introduced to Captain Ball, sworn in and congratulated on being the first QA to join that army unit. This didn't mean a lot to me at the time. Later, however, when I received my army number (Q1000 364), I realised that I was the first QA in the northern region. I was attached to the Royal Army Medical Corps TA, 1st Northern General Hospital.

Although there were QAs in the Second World War the girls were all officers and State Registered Nurses. After the war, someone decided there should also be other ranks and this is where I came in.

Before long there were about a dozen of us, and in a short space of time our unit grew to over 300 people, including doctors, dentists, pharmacists, nurses and about 100 ex-National Servicemen. When National Servicemen completed their two years' conscription they then did three years as Z reservists, which meant they had to attend an annual TA camp and a number of evening drills.

One of the National Servicemen acted as storeman/driver and he later became my husband. As storeman his duties included checking the stock of uniforms each day. Uniforms for ladies included regulation army bloomers, but no-one ever wore them.

In my regular job I worked as a clerk in the Ministry at Longbenton. I went to the TA two nights a week where I spent my time doing a bit of typing and going to lectures on various aspects of nursing in wartime. I also had a lot of fun and met people from all walks of life – nurses, doctors, bus drivers and miners.

Our first annual camp was at Catterick Army Hospital and we all hated it! The food was atrocious and we had to get up at 6.00 am to be on the wards at 7.00. Fortunately subsequent camps were much better. For lots of young girls like me, the TA opened up a whole new world. I had never travelled further than Alnwick, but with the TA I went all over the country to places like Cambridge, Chester, London, the Isle of Wight and Ireland. Life was never dull!

Mabs Taylor

A man's wage

My first job was at Dillons, a market garden in Woolsington. I stayed there until 1952 when I went into the RAF. When I went back to Dillons after my National Service they were only offering £5 a week, but my pals were all working on building sites where you could get £15 or £20 a week. So I went on the building sites, and built some of the new estates including Wideopen. After that I worked for Carrick's as a salesman with a van. You bought your own stock from Carrick's and if you sold it you made a profit. If you didn't sell it you had to throw it away – you couldn't give it back. Carrick's had over 100 vans coming out of the bakery from 6 o'clock in the morning.

Joseph Luke

Joseph Luke

Joseph in his Carrick's van, late 1950s.

A model employee

In the early 1950s, Auntie Joan worked at the art department at King's College in Newcastle. She was a nude model. She had no inhibitions. My mother saw the job in the paper and said 'Look Joan there's a job here. Wonderful money!' After that she went to Chelsea College of Art in London and modelled for famous artists. She knew Quentin Crisp and other celebrities. She had lovely paintings, very valuable, from people who were just students when she knew them, including David Hockney. Someone took a life size photo of her. My grandma had never seen any thing as lewd in her life. 'You call it art,' she said. 'I can think of a worse name!'

When she came to visit us from London she wore a black hat with a great big feather, and elegant black and white fitted jacket and a pencil slim black skirt. We lived in a council street and everyone was staring at her. She looked like someone out of a painting!

Pauline Luke and Mary McArdle

First jobs

When I was still at school I worked at the Tatler restaurant on Northumberland Street, just to get some pocket money. I had to wear black but I didn't have any black clothes so I had to buy something specially. I wore a man's stiff collar pinned to my hair as a hat. The other waitresses were all older; they were Irish and hard as nails. The restaurant had a grand piano and a lovely piano player. It served food I'd never heard of like Spaghetti Bolognese and big Knickerbocker Glories. They hired the Tatler out to a jazz club on Wednesday nights.

Norah Coombes

In the 1950s the North East coast, especially Whitley Bay, enjoyed an influx of Scots holiday-makers during the high summer months. To cater for their entertainment needs the Theatre Royal in Newcastle put on a comedy revue usually starring the popular Scots comedian Chic Murray (and Pip Hinton).

Seeking vacation work, my friend Peter and I, emboldened by a pint or two at the Crow's Nest in the Haymarket, wandered down to the stage door in Shakespeare Street and asked if there were any vacancies, anticipating the possibility of cleaning or even ushering jobs. 'Sorry' was the immediate response, but after a short pause 'But we do need a couple of electricians.' I knew how to switch on a light but Peter had been trained as a radar technician during his National Service and promptly asserted that we could fulfil that role. His RAF experience was accepted without hesitation but they never bothered to ask about my qualification!

Peter was assigned to the main lighting console where he was required to manage house and stage lighting according to a script related to the frequently changing scenes or sketches in the show. My task was to run on stage between each of these and, with another script, plug in any electrical items that were required. I had to co-ordinate with the stage hands who carried on items of furniture.

Dead easy – money for old rope, except that we were working with some crazy people, led, of course, by Chic Murray himself. They would do everything they could think of to subvert our scripted activity.

A favourite trick was to impede our work so that, as Peter raised the curtain according to his script, I was exposed on stage to the delight of the audience and also to Chic because it gave him an opportunity to improvise and raise a huge gale of laughter.

Even when out of sight hiding behind a sofa I was kicked by the performers every time they had to move to that position. Of course, they made it so obvious that the audience was fully aware of what was happening.

We were paid a modest sum for each performance and double time for rehearsals on Sundays when the show changed for the following week. It was the best vacation job we ever had!

Brian Sefton

We lived very protected lives – too protected – I left home in 1956 and went to London, worked as a secretary, then became an advertising copywriter, and joined the swinging sixties.

Jane Jantet

Looking up Northumberland Street in 1956. The Tatler was near the top on the left. Amos Atkinson's shoe shop, far right, had been elaborately decorated with plasterwork for the Coronation in 1953.

There were plenty of jobs for men to apply for at the Employment Exchange as this advertisement from The Journal, February 1952, shows.

There was not quite as much choice for women!

The Night Road North (extract from the Thomas Hedley 'Moonbeams' magazine, 1953)

'The large doors of Newcastle Factory's loading bay are slid back. A blaze of light streams out into the early morning darkness of City Road. The time is one am. The street is deserted. Above the low hum of factory machinery there is a sharper noise – a van starts up and moves from the bay into the street.

SITUATIONS VACANT

Openings available for

MEN

Ships' Plumbers, Wood Cutting Machinists, Riveting Squads (Machine), Rivet Heaters, Red Leaders, Constructional Platers, Patternmakers, Moulders (All Types), Coremakers, Blacksmiths, Blacksmiths' Strikers, Electric Welders, Burners, Coppersmiths, Sheet Metal Workers, Fitters (Engineering and Marine), Motor Mechanics, Mechanic-Examiners, Turners, Engineering Machinists (All Types, Skilled and Semi-Skilled), French Polishers, Glass Makers, Bus Drivers and Conductors, Weavers, Draughtsmen, Police Constables.

WOMEN

Shorthand-Typists (Senior and Junior), Daily and Residential Cooks.

Full details of these and other jobs at the

EMPLOYMENT EXCHANGE

IN EACH DISTRICT OF TYNESIDE

" MINISTRY OF LABOUR AND NATIONAL SERVICE

Procter & Gamble

The driver is Prideaux Patterson. With a 'Goodnight' to Joe Davidson the night watchman, he drives away, through the strangely quiet main street of Newcastle towards the North Road. Street lamps are on but their light reveals only one or two people still up and out – a policeman checking that shop doors are locked, two young men walking home from a dance. With so few people about the street seems wider, the buildings higher. Prideaux's destination is Berwick. His load is five tons of Hedley products.'

Driver Prideaux Patterson, right, enjoys a cup of Oxo at a transport café in Morpeth.

Only You

The Platters, 1955

Getting married

On New Year's Eve, 1957, I was invited to friend's house. She lived in St Thomas' Street and we went to the dance at the Milvain on Westgate Road. Here we met two soldiers who were on leave. One was a local boy whose mother lived in Heaton and we all went back to my friend's house for a drink to bring in the New Year. I arranged to meet this boy to go to the cinema the next day and when his leave was up we wrote to each other. He was the boy I married.

We were married in September 1958 at St Margaret's Church on Armstrong Road. The weather was good. My reception was held at the Eldon Grill near the Monument where we had a sit down meal for 28 people and my husband and I paid for all of it. After the reception we went to the Central Station and caught a train at the start of our journey to the Isle of Wight. My mother in law invited any of the guests to join her at her home for a drink and a nibble. My bridesmaid was Maureen, a girl I worked with in the Co-op, she wore blue – a dress she had borrowed! My brother in law gave me away.

Mary Dodds

I wore a dress made by one of the Murray House members. I chose the material at Fenwick's – a pale cream heavy brocade.

225

In December 1958 I flew to Germany, where my husband was stationed, to spend Christmas with him and his friend's family. I flew from Woolsington Airport, which at that time consisted of wooden huts. However the Co-op wasn't keen on employing married women so they would not let me have extra leave to go to Germany. I went without pay and had to put in my notice when I returned.

Mary Dodds

Mum and Dad were Newcastle Central Methodist's Church's first Chinese members and their 1957 wedding was a newsworthy story. The photographer who was booked for the wedding failed to turn up – later they discovered that he had been burgled. The minister quickly contacted the newspapers to see if someone could come and take pictures. Dad often said that if the minister had not been so quick thinking, they would not have had any pictures of the wedding at all. Mum and Dad were introduced by my Aunt Letty (Mum's cousin). They started off as pen pals. Letty is in the photo (just behind Dad) and was a bridesmaid at the wedding. Money was tight and Mum's wedding dress and veil were lent to her by Marjorie Chen, but she bought her own headdress of wax flowers. Sometime after the wedding the photographer did take some photos of Mum and Dad (wearing their wedding finery) in his studio. I remember as a child never quite understanding why Mum had a different, very inferior bouquet in these pictures!

Grace Shaw

Virginia Yuet Yung Chiu (meaning Bright Full Moon) marries Samuel Tak Shing Wong (meaning Success), August 1957.

Angela Merritt, Grace Shaw

I was born in May 1952, in our home at Back Shields Road, Byker, above Cook's Pork Shop. I was the youngest of 11 children; my eldest brother Peter was born in 1930. I wasn't the youngest in the family for long because four of my sisters were married in the 1950s. Rita, Audrey, Vida and May soon began having families of their own. I was only ten months old when Rita, my eldest sister, was married at St Silas Church, Byker

Audrey's wedding at St Silas Church, Byker, 1957. Derek (looking uncomfortable in his best suit!) with his mam, dad and brother are on the right of the picture.

and according to Vida, who was put in charge of me, I cried all day.

The only sister whose wedding I can remember was Audrey, who married Alan Franklin in 1957 when I was five years old. She was also married at St Silas Church, where we were all christened. Alan was from Hebburn, so we travelled in wedding cars where a second ceremony was performed in his local church. My late brother John was best man. Mam, dad and I were the only guests from Audrey's side. I can remember Audrey being annoyed because someone had buttoned my suit jacket on the wrong side. We had a lovely day and my parents were so proud of my big sister and her new husband.

Derek Steele

227

The hoy oot

My memory of weddings on Scotswood Rd was the 'hoy oot' when handfuls of pennies would be thrown when the bride left the house. All of the bairns in the neighbourhood would scrabble to try and collect as much brass as possible. When a christening party walked home (very few people had cars in the 50s) from the church the mother would gift the first child they met with a piece of christening cake and a silver sixpence.

Stephen Charlton

Patricia Bensdorp Clark

A wedding in 1951 in Gosforth. I am the bridesmaid on the far left and my aunt made all the dresses herself as she was a dressmaker. The reception was at a hired hall on Gosforth High Street. I was at the Sacred Heart Convent and as we were Catholics we had to get permission from Canon Wilkinson at the RC St Mary's Cathedral to take part in a Protestant service! Patricia Bensdorp Clark

Rock Around the Clock

Bill Haley and the Comets, 1954

Popular music and all that jazz

Johnny Handle's jazz debut

I had been having piano lessons since 1943 to little avail; I was not destined to be a music reader. However by 1948 I had discovered that I could pick up melodies from the wireless and play them by ear. By 1950, I had acquired a repertoire of popular dance tunes of the time, plus a good number of 'standards' from the past and was called upon to entertain at youth clubs in the east of Newcastle.

I soon discovered jazz and finding some kindred spirits at school (Heaton Grammar) we formed The Barbary Jazz Band in 1951/52. I think we did a couple of gigs for students before breaking up as members left school. Joe Young (the banjo player who became famous later as a band leader) came out to school to hear us practise and told us where we could hear jazz.

One of the venues was

Johnny Handle (kneeling) and fellow band members at Rye Hill youth club around 1951 or 1952.

Johnny Handle/ncjMedia Ltd

the Newcastle Jazz Club at the Socialist Hall, Royal Arcade, Pilgrim Street. This was basically a dance hall with a stage and no alcohol, only light refreshments.

Most of the people were a few years older than us, some more so, and spent the evening jiving to the resident bands, The Panama, The Bernicia and the High Society Jazzmen. Some of the musicians in the audience were asked to play to give the resident musicians a rest.

Occasionally they would book guest artists. I heard blues singers Bill Broonzy and Josh White there.

We heard that Rutherford Technical College hired out their refectory one evening a week to bands for rehearsal. We investigated and were pleasantly surprised to hear quite good quality jazz from The Castle and the Louisiana Band. I had a 'sit in' with the Louisiana Band, and was later asked to join them when Clem Avery vacated the piano stool and

Johnny Handle (piano) with Clem Avery's Band, 1954 at Heaton Alexandria Club. Joe Young is on banjo.

took up the trumpet. By 1953 we had secured a residency at Blaydon Conservative club, and began to rehearse at the Labour Club rooms in Percy Street on Saturday afternoons. It was quite a parade when we came out with our brown band shirts with yellow ribbon on the pockets, and LJB in large capitals across the front. We strolled through the shopping crowds following John Franklin wearing his huge sousaphone with the band logo stenciled across the bell.

In 1951 I met a clarinet and saxophone player from Heaton called Colin Beal. We started to do gigs together. Colin was able to play jazz and dance band tunes, so we often got functions where we could combine the music (and get paid). This musical association lasted until National Service intervened in the late 1950s. We had certain regular bookings, often on a monthly basis. I remember doing the Delecta

Hall in Raby Street with Eric Oakley on drums and Brian O'Byrne duetting with Colin on clarinets. The piano was so far out of tune, they had to pull out their mouthpieces and barrel joints to stay in pitch, with the result that they came apart during the rendition of *The Red Flag* (it was a Young Communists' social) Another regular one was the Newcastle Airport dinner dance. Very posh. People used to fly in for it on their light aircraft.

Clem Avery formed a new Band in 1954 and asked me to play piano with him. It was a great swinging group, and we found a rather decayed Gentlemen's Club on Heaton Road (Alexandra Jazz Club), which was keen to rent us their concert room. It had a grand piano, so I enjoyed playing there.

I used to do ragtime and blues spots in the intervals as well as playing with the group. After a year in Heaton, Clem left the band to go in the Services.

Joe Young (banjo) took over the band, renamed it the Mighty Joe Young Band, and I played trumpet.

Soon Joe was keen on going towards mainstream jazz, and when John Walters joined the front line, for a while there were two trumpets. The Downbeat Club was the new trendy jazz venue, and more and more people came to listen, rather than dancing to the music. I preferred the more 'Trad' stuff, and formed a band, with

Johnny Handle

Colin Beal's band, Rye Hill youth club, 1955. Colin Beal is on clarinet, Johnny Handle on trumpet, Jack Goodwin on trombone, David Reed on banjo, Chas Coles on drums.

231

John Saxelby on clarinet, called the Levee Ramblers.

For about nine months we had a weekly jazz club at the Marlborough Social club until John got head hunted by the prestigious Zenith Six band at Manchester. Around this time, due to call-ups for the military and people leaving the North for work or university, band populations would fluctuate. A lot of us had common repertoires of standard jazz tunes, so this did not cause too much trouble. Quite often you would be required to take up a different instrument to fill a vacancy.

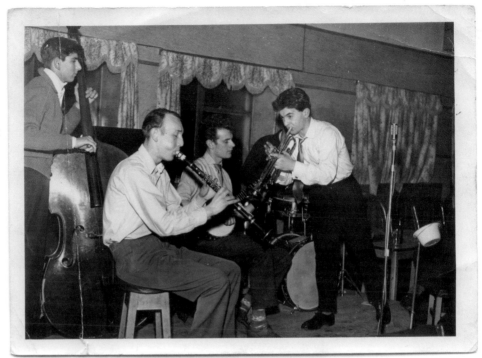

The Levee Ramblers perform at Marlborough Jazz Club, 1956.

After the Levee Ramblers split up, I began working more regularly with Colin and band size varied according to the engagements. We had his 'Big' band for Chester-le-Street dance hall with eight members, a six piece for jazz and a Trio/ Quartet for the smaller (and more frequent events). By 1957 jazz was popular and with the skiffle craze there seemed to be music gigs five nights out of seven!

Another source of work at this time was being resident pianist at pubs and clubs. I worked at Heaton, Blaydon, Whitley Bay and Dudley, backing singers, concert parties, or just doing background music between the bingo sessions. Quite a baptism of fire … you had to be able to play with or without music in any key.

By 1958 I was doing a lot of singing with guitar and banjo. The New Orleans Club in Shieldfield was well established as a Jazz Co-operative venue, and we started a folk and blues evening that led to the folk club movement starting on Tyneside. For a year I joined the Vieux Caree Band at this club, on double bass but by then the folksong revival was gathering strength so I moved away from the jazz to a new interest – local songs and tunes.

Johnny Handle

Mahogany Hall Stomp

I was chairman of Newcastle Jazz Club in the 1950s. Every Tuesday night we stomped at Mahogany Hall in the old Royal Arcade at the foot of Pilgrim Street.

The venue was originally the Socialist Hall and I had to go before City Magistrates to justify my reasons for changing the name to something more appropriate. Mahogany Hall was a legendary venue on Basin Street, New Orleans, built in 1897.

Two remarkable evenings were the appearance of Big Bill Broonzy on 1 November 1955 and Josh White two weeks later. Big Bill was the last of the great traditional Country Blues singers who appeared on stage in the clothes in which he travelled whereas Josh, who was a City Blues and folk singer, changed twice (even down to his socks) during his performance (no, not on stage). Big Bill carried a bottle of 'vocal lubricant' in his guitar case whereas Josh had stage shoes in his.

Dobson's Royal Arcade was demolished in 1964 to make way for the urban motorway. The stone lay on spare land in Byker for some years and I rescued three small ones, which are now in my rockery. I swear, on a still night, when the moon is right, if I stand near the Aubrietia I can faintly hear Mahogany Hall Stomp.

Alan Brown

Shake Rattle and Roll

Rock Around the Clock came out in 1954 in America and was here by 1955. So it was the dawn of rock and roll. Bill Haley came to the Odeon in 1957, but my first influences were jazz and I was a bit reluctant to associate myself with this crude new music! I regret that!

The first place to hear live jazz (my older brother already listened to Fats Waller and British Dixieland stuff) was in the Royal Arcade at the foot of Pilgrim Street. It was a fantastic old building that went all the way through from Pilgrim Street and down stone steps to Manors. Just before you went down the stairs to Manors there was a door on the left that led upstairs to a room that went right across the width of the building and that was the first Newcastle Jazz Club. Local musicians played there, like Johnny Handle. He played trumpet and piano at the same time, one hand on each! The Panama Jazzmen were the top jazz band then. Mighty Joe Young was starting out – by the late Fifties he was top of the heap and would give my little band the interval spot at the University Jazz Club on Blackett Street, Mike Jeffery's first musical venture.

When I got to art school in 1956 the New Orleans Club opened on Melbourne Street in Shieldfield. It was a pretty derelict building. There was long room, with a bar at one end and a stage at the other, which could fit 100 people. It was packed on a Saturday night when The Mighty Joe Young Jazzmen were resident. Some nights there'd be 20 of our gang hanging out there.

There was a split between people who were into jazz and those who were into rock and roll. There was a split within the jazz fans too! You were either a traddie or a modernist. I had got in with an older crowd at Gateshead Grammar School and they introduced me to jazz concerts at the City Hall. They were strictly New Orleans and Chicago jazz. But at art school there was a modernist crowd who took me under their wing, so I got converted to modern jazz; the high priests were Charlie Parker and Dizzy Gillespie, Charles Mingus, Thelonious Monk and Miles Davis from the east coast school of jazz. Then cool school emerged on the west coast; The Gerry Mulligan Quartet with Chet Baker, Shorty Rogers's Giants, Zoot Sims, Stan Getz and Dave Brubeck. So then there was a schism between hard bop on the east coast, and the cool school on the west coast. Eventually you began to realise that it was just all music.

I hate the word Dixieland but I loved people like Louis Armstrong, Jelly Roll Morton and Bix Beiderbecke. There was a ridiculous Musicians' Union ban that wouldn't allow American musicians to come over here in case they undermined British musicians' jobs. But they did see the light after about 1956. Stan Kenton was the first American band to come over under the new rules. Then American bands

Rock and Roll king Bill Haley and the Comets at Newcastle's Odeon in February 1957.

I saw Bill Haley, who came to the Odeon Cinema in Pilgrim Street to give a live performance. The ticket cost me £1, which was a considerable amount when you consider my annual Student Grant was £232 plus fees from the West Riding County Council. (They were generous: if you came from Cheshire as one of my friends did, you got £180 plus fees). I also used to go to Chris Barber and Humphrey Lyttelton concerts. Tony Finn

It was just so different, the joyousness of it … something new, the Odeon just erupted! Anne Taylor started to come over regularly. Stan Kenton (who I didn't go to see because he was a modernist. I've regretted that ever since), Louis Armstrong, Lionel Hampton, George Lewis, Count Basie. This was all within months of getting to art school. The first live band I ever saw was Mick Mulligan with a young George Melly. Second concert was Louis Armstrong. The downside was that the American promoters put a variety show on with him. One of the acts was a peg leg dancer who did hoofing with his wooden leg … good … but not what we wanted! The City Hall was packed out. The man himself, Louis Armstrong – trumpet and vocals, Edmund Hall – clarinet, Trummy Young – trombone, Billy Kyle – piano, Arville Shaw – bass and Barrett Deems – drums. Awesome!

After that I saw everyone who came … brilliant stuff and a fabulous atmosphere. They had a good no smoking policy, which was unusual at the time, and even as a smoker it was nice – you could see what was going on. At the interval everyone poured out into the lobby for a smoke and a chance to discuss the show so far. At about 10pm we'd go to the pub, the Northumberland Arms, or the Crow's Nest. At first I was too young for the pub but I was inspired. I took up trumpet first, to have a shot at jazz. Not focussed. Just for fun. I could only play in b flat, very basic!

At art school I met Eric Burdon and hit it off straight away. We formed The Pagan Jazzmen. I was on trumpet and Eric on trombone, with a couple of friends of his, Alan Sanderson on snare drum and high hat and Jimmy Crawford on banjo. We started practising at Jimmy's place. We were just 16. And then we started practising at my house which had a big upstairs room above our two shops.

John Steel

The Pagan Jazzmen at a dance in Byker in 1959. Left to right: Eric Burdon, John Steel, David Ashcroft, Philip Payne, Jimmy Crawford.

There was a youth club at nearby Felling and we asked if we could get up and play at the hop night, for nothing. We did a handful of numbers, playing in front of people. Scary! They were a bit bemused … Eric couldn't really play the trombone, but the banjo and high hat were a bit more competent. That lasted about a year at the most. But by this time rock and roll had taken over!

Lonnie Donegan started it all with the skiffle craze. He recorded Rock Island Line in 1956. Everyone just went 'whoa … get a guitar, learn three chords, off you go'. It was a different strand to Bill Haley's American rock and roll. He was ahead with his rock-a-billy beat and rhythm and blues influence. Haley did *Shake Rattle and Roll* (the first record I ever bought), which was a cover of Joe Turner. It was Kansas City Jazz. I bought it from a shop on Gateshead High Street, and after that I'd buy from Windows and Jeavons (Percy Street and Pudding Chare). I bought my first drums from Kitchen's on Ridley Place. There were so many influences. Elvis came along with *Heartbreak Hotel*. Bill Haley mostly appealed to boys but Elvis really appealed to the girls too. There was Fats Domino, Little Richard, Jerry Lee Lewis, Chuck Berry. They were our hard core rock and roll heroes. There were also the copyists of Elvis, like Pat Boon, the younger good looking white boys covering the black American songs and making commercial hits, and the excellent Everly Brothers. We were caught up in it all.

We had a sudden turnaround because of all this. Eric said he wanted to get into rock and roll and decided to sing, Jimmy the banjo player said he'd play electric guitar, Alan the drummer wanted to play bass guitar and got one of the first bass guitars, so I said I'd play the drums. We were then the Pagans. It was a good name!

CITY HALL,
Northumberland Road, Newcastle-on-Tyne, 1.
Saturday, May 4th, 1957, at 7.30 p.m.
ALAN J. BROWN
Presents
THE VIPERS SKIFFLE GROUP
THE GATEWAY JAZZ BAND
THE PANAMA JAZZMEN
AREA 5/-
(Tax Inclusive)
SEAT M 15
Booking Agents: Waddington & Sons Ltd., Metrovick House, Northumberland Road, Newcastle-on-Tyne, 1.
This Portion to be Retained
Phillips Printers Ltd., Trafalgar St., Newcastle-on-Tyne, 1.

City Hall

J. STEEL
Tel. Low Fell 76257
PAGAN JAZZ MEN
DISCORDANT, SYNCOPATED MUSIC AT YOUR DISPOSAL

John Steel

The high water mark for this line up was an appearance on *The Carroll Levis Discovery Show* at the Newcastle Empire Theatre. This was the forerunner of *Opportunity Knocks* and all of the talent discovery shows since. It was on its last legs by this time, as was variety theatre in general, because of the relatively new competition from television. The man himself no longer compered the shows but instead used minor celebrities and 'starlets' to MC the proceedings. On this round of the circuit we had Joan Collins'

Not the best of shots from the Empire balcony, but a rare and historic view of the Pagan Jazz Men in concert on the Carroll Levis Discovery Show!

stunning little sister, then about 22 years old, and later to become much more famous as Jackie Collins, the author of sexy Hollywood novels. She walked on wearing a very tight fitting dress with extreme décolletage and introduced us – our first time on the big stage. We didn't win but it was fun and I did learn something useful. None of us had been on stage in a theatre before, and we were surprised to find that there was a distinct slope from the back of the stage down to the footlights. This was so that the action at the back could be seen by the people sitting in the stalls, of course. After that, I always made sure that my drums were firmly anchored, as on this occasion I was in a sweat all through our number as the kit crept steadily towards the orchestra pit.

Our name changed to the Kansas City 5 then Kansas City 7, then the Alan Price Rhythm and Blues Combo. We used to see EmCee 5 a lot, they were brilliant, and eventually I played in a trio with Mike Carr at the A Go Go on weekday nights. They had two brilliant professional musicians who'd play for Don Smith at the Oxford Galleries in the big band. One was Ronnie Stephenson from Sunderland – drums, the other Barry Cox from Glasgow – tenor sax.

John Steel

Music began to play a part in my life at the end of the 1950s. My dad played the mandolin and piano and I was starting to take trumpet lessons. My older cousin Neil, who lived on Netherby Drive, Fenham, was a teenager into rock and roll. He had brown leather winklepickers and greased back hair – it was at his house that for the first time I heard a heavy backbeat in music, very exciting. Soon my older brother Keith had a record player in our bedroom and was playing Buddy Holly, Eddie Cochran and Chuck Berry 45s. That would later lead us to American blues and folk music. We sometimes went to the Spanish City, Whitley Bay, on the train, where the same music was played really loud on the dodgems and the waltzer.

Carl Gustafson

The Larry Williams Look

During the late Fifties, like many young boys growing up in Newcastle, I watched with envy as my older brother and his friends would don their Teddy Boy outfits (long, Edwardian style jackets and tight trousers in garish colours, made to measure at Jackson's the Tailor, worn with crepe soled shoes and sported with a greased-back, quiffed hairstyle) and sashay down to their local hangouts (or wherever they were allowed to hang out) for a night of smoking, jiving, and most of all, posing with their girlfriends to a background of rock and roll music.

Too young to be a part of this fledgling scene, I took consolation in being allowed to listen to his record collection while my brother was out, under pain of death not to damage or break any of the 78-rpm discs that were his pride and joy.

One Friday night in 1957, when I was ten years old, I was listening to his latest acquisition – a rock and roll record called *Bony Moronie*, sung by Larry Williams, recorded on the London label and bought from Windows in the Central Arcade for the princely sum of six shillings and eightpence.

I'm now a mature student of this musical genre and know that this record was a typical product of the New Orleans sound, majoring on driving piano, fat drums, wailing sax and powerful vocals, featuring studio musicians who also played on records by Fats Domino and Little Richard.

However, I didn't know any of this then – I just thought it was a giant of a record, with a powerful sound, crazy vocals and funny lyrics, and I admired my brother's musical taste in buying it.

Imagine my delight then, when on opening my brother's other major purchase of that week, his copy of the *New Musical Express*, there before me was a picture of my new idol: Larry Williams.

Now Larry was a young black singer from New Orleans, judging by the photograph about 6ft 2ins tall, and was wearing a white suit and a pair of black and white two-tone shoes. But what got me was the hair – a magnificent black pompadour, greased and combed back into what was then fashionably called a DA, with a sheen that would put a newly waxed car to shame.

That was it – my bad hair days were over! Never mind that my hair was pale, fair and lank, once it was brylcreemed up and swept back in the Larry style, I would conquer all before me, and I immediately set about my follicular transformation. I wondered what to do about my spectacles, which gave me a quiet, studious look, but since I needed them to see what I was doing to my hair in the mirror, I decided to leave them on.

I must have looked absolutely and utterly ridiculous, but to my enthusiastic gaze and fevered imagination, my hair was now a masterpiece. Examined from every angle, and definitely passing muster as my home town's contribution to the rock and roll hall of fame, I paraded my new look out onto the sidewalk. Well, the back garden, actually.

Our neighbour, Mrs Rule, a kindly, inquisitive old soul, who happened to be hanging the washing out, glanced across, a look of bafflement spreading across her features, and said, 'Hello Terry, what have you done to your hair?'

'It's a Larry Williams style', I replied, matter of factly.

There was a slight pause.

'Ooh', she said, and nodded in bewilderment.

After a moment Mr Rule popped his head out of the door, turned my way and stared for a full ten seconds before asking:

'Terry, what have you done to your hair lad?'

This was promptly answered by Mrs Rule, who piped up, 'Actually, it's a Larry Williams style, dear'.

Her husband paused, nodded, and plodded back into the house, totally bemused.

I don't know whether they immediately forgot about Larry, or spent the rest of the night wondering who on earth he was. They certainly wouldn't have realized the profound effect that his sort of music would have on thousands of kids like me, and English musicians during the next decade, the Beatles, for instance. But I conjure up an image of Mr Rule going down to the pub later that night and asking his cronies, 'Ever heard of a bloke called Larry Williams?' 'Larry Williams? Never heard of him. Does he live round here?' 'Haven't a clue', replies Mr. Rule, 'but you'll know him if you see him – he's got the worst haircut you've ever seen!'

Terry Goulding

Some of the members and guests of Rye Hill Youth Club at their Christmas party round the juke box, which was hired for the night, in December 1957.

The City Hall

Newcastle City Hall hosted a huge variety of musical and other performances during the 1950s, ranging from the most famous orchestras such at the Hallé and the London Philharmonic to light music of all kinds, jazz (trad and modern), skiffle, and rock and roll. Performers included Dame Myra Hess in May 1954, Johnny Dankworth the same year, Ella Fitzgerald in 1955 (and later years), Tyneside Jazz Festival (April 1955), the Liverpool Philharmonic, Jimmy Shand, the Rock n Roll Sinners (1957), the Vipers Skiffle Group, Glasgow Phoenix Choir, Count Basie, Buddy Holly (1958), Tommy Steele, Paul Robeson, Cliff Richard (1959), and of course the Northern Sinfonia. The list runs into many hundreds. Newcastle music fans of all kinds were well catered for.

Apparently in 1954 the City Hall did turn down Nat King Cole as 'jazz fans are rowdy', but he would appear there in later years.

Ella Fitzgerald and Oscar Peterson arrive at Newcastle Airport 1 March 1955 en route to their performance at the City Hall. There to meet them (right) was Jim Denyer, the manager of the airport.

Singer Frankie Vaughan in a record shop in Percy Street, probably Jeavons, to sign autographs for his adoring teenage fans 6 March 1954.

It's Almost Tomorrow

The Dream Weavers, 1955

The student life

Going to Art College

In 1958 I went to Newcastle College of Art and Industrial design. I was 15. There was a prelim course, which covered a broad spectrum of subjects and then a two-year intermediate course, similar to today's foundation course. I was headed for the fashion department, which was then a two-year degree course, three years if you missed the intermediate course.

We were in a big hurry to fit into college life so on the Saturday of Rag Week, we got onto the college float. Apparently it was a Viking ship and, in keeping with the Viking experience, Johnny Steel (of the Animals fame) played the theme tune from the Vikings film (with Kirk Douglas and Tony Curtis) most of the day on his trumpet. We went on a

Elspeth Rutter

Elspeth and friends, 1959. Eddie and Walter were supposed to wear shirts and ties to college, but Eddie is being rebellious.

long route round Newcastle then down the Coast Road to Whitley Bay and back through Walker and Byker, collecting for charity all the way. All the shop girls on Shields Road were shouting and waving to Eric Burdon who was a Byker lad and obviously very popular.

The college was in a large old mansion on Clayton Road in Jesmond. It housed painting, fashion, fabric printing, pottery, life drawing, graphics and photography. There were outbuildings in the grounds at the back for industrial design, furniture design and exhibition design. Lithography and the big old type printing machines were at Bath Lane. My future husband, Alan, did print studies there on the graphic design course. Then as the college grew, it spread more and more, and we had the use of old school buildings off Chillingham Road. We did life drawing, painting, photography and graphic design there. I remember a Persian student started the intermediate course there, and he had a transistor radio from America, we were all very impressed as it was the first one we had ever seen.

Elspeth Rutter

Art students in the graphic design studio.

Rag Week

Rag week was great. For a couple of years I was on the rag floats, as we (at the art school) were affiliated to King's College. I played trumpet in the streets and wore a fedora hat and a long black coat with a flower in my button hole. Did we really go all the way to Morpeth and back? I remember doing that. People threw coins onto the float and it was really painful to get hit with an old copper penny.

In 1956 or 1957 our art school float was a Viking long boat. We needed a mast so we stopped a 33 trolley bus on the road on the corner of Clayton Road. While we were talking to the conductor, a couple of the gang swiped the great long pole that ran underneath the bus. It was used to hook the bus poles back on the wires when they fell off. They hauled it out while the conductor was distracted and ran off with it down the road. That became our mascot on the Viking long ship.

John Steel

King's College Rag Week, held during the third week in October, was one of the major events of the academic year. Rag Week was in its prime during the 1950s and King's was always at the top of the league in raising money for charity, largely due the generosity of the people of Tyneside. My room mate and I volunteered to run the Rag transport. Companies around Tyneside lent us a variety of vehicles for the week, which ended with big procession through the streets of Newcastle and surrounding areas A group of trainee teachers from Kenton Lodge teacher training college formed a skiffle group to help us raise money. We drove them around the pubs of Newcastle while they performed the music of Lonnie Donegan.

George and I embarked on this mission with some

Henderson Hall skiffle group, 1957.

fear and trepidation considering that we were transporting eight attractive young ladies in a somewhat ancient lorry, loaned by Newcastle Brewery, visiting pubs full of Geordies who had already put away a few pints. The outcome was very successful. We did this most nights of Rag week and always managed to finish up with the same eight young ladies.

Rag Week was a time for riotous behaviour. There would usually be a raid on Edinburgh University with the objective of stealing the union mascot. Along

Martin Nellist

I think it was the Medics' idea, in 1957, to put a young lady in a foam bath on the back of a truck and taking her around the streets with collecting tins. They are setting up outside the Union. Martin Nellist

Northumberland Street there was one shop that had a figure of a naked lady suspended across the pavement some fifteen feet above the ground. This provided a challenge for the college mountain climbing club, who climbed the building during the night and dressed the statute in scanty underwear. Another stunt was when someone cemented a complete toilet into the pavement in Northumberland Street using quick setting cement. By the time it was found it was not easy to remove.

Anthony Weeden

I took part in the Rag Reviews, which were public performances at the theatre in the Haymarket - sometimes with a bit of difficulty. Using the theatre orchestra was part of the deal, but we had no rehearsals with them until the dress rehearsal, when the tempo they had rehearsed (separately) wasn't always the tempo we were expecting. It's not easy to tap to a different time scale at short notice.

The rag procession came at the end of rag week and was always very well supported by the townspeople. The geology department constructed a large dinosaur one year. It had to be almost completely dismantled to get it up onto the lorry, which of course was busy delivering beer until the morning of the big day. Not that it was delivering to the Students' Union – their Newcastle Brown came by tanker. We had several sheepskins as costumes and large marrow bones to wield. I led the dinosaur with a very thin piece of string round its long overhanging neck but I had to scurry, especially up Westgate Road., as even at slowest speed a huge lorry travels surprising quickly.

Judith Wells (née Sellers)

Martin Nellist

Girls from Ethel Williams Hall conduct a keep-fit session in the Haymarket, 1957.

Martin Nellist

The Agrics Wolf of 1957 was constructed from papier mâché and was made at the rear of the old Agric building. We were immediately adjacent to the Architects with whom there was much rivalry. One night some Architects took the almost completed wolf and towed it to Holy Island, where they intended that it would be cut off by the tide. However, we used one of the Departmental vehicles to chase after them and managed to reach Holy Island and retrieve the wolf just in time. At least two of the Architects were caught and, I think, taken back to Newcastle in the Departmental vehicle. This gave me the opportunity to make a small contribution to this escapade when, as the only one with a driving licence, I drove the Architects' old Austin 7 back to Newcastle. We didn't worry about insurance!

Martin Nellist

Rag Charities Week was a fun-filled time for many students. The event was a great fundraiser and over £16,000 was collected in 1959. I (Bill Stephenson) remember playing a genuine Boer War bugle in the 1959 Rag Band, which used to march from the Union Building each day to lead student collectors into the Newcastle streets. I could blow little more than a raspberry, but no-one seemed to care.

In those far-off days, Northumberland Street formed part of the A1, the main London to Edinburgh highway. It was always jammed with traffic and shoppers on Saturday mornings – the perfect time to fill the street with students seeking donations. The situation was helped on one occasion by Peter Thurley who arranged to have his Rolls Royce break down in the midst of this traffic jam.

Crowds gathered as he feigned attempts to coax his car back to life. He was helped by various policemen. His was not the only car to breakdown. Several were diagonally parked on the highway along the length of the main thoroughfare. That was when the students descended to extract cash from unsuspecting shoppers.

These crowds were very good-natured and had a high tolerance level for students from King's.

IT'S A MYSTERY...OR IS IT?

Electrical students suspected

ONLY two people shared the secret of how a rough white "flag" reached the top of a mast on Carliol House, the electricity centre, in Newcastle, yesterday.

They are believed to be electrical engineering students who hoisted it as an unofficial Rag stunt.

The caretaker of the six-storey building said last night: "I don't know how it got there, but it arrived during the afternoon and I soon had it down. It seemed to be made from a bed sheet and just had the word RAG daubed on it in creosote."

The vice-president of Rag Central Committee, Mr. I. R. Sutherland, said last night: "This was an unofficial stunt. We did not know about it. I think it was accomplished by some electrical engineering students."

Official stunts which amused shoppers and motorists in the city yesterday included a "strip-tease act" in Northumberland Street, a wind-screen wiping service by some oddly attired attendants at the Haymarket traffic lights, and a game of hockey in Clayton Street.

The Mystery Flag

Sidney Emerson was in charge of unofficial stunts in 1959 and organized several exciting raids. On the afternoon of Wednesday, 21 October (Trafalgar Day) the Electricity Board HQ, Carliol House, was raided and a makeshift flag bearing the Rag symbol was eventually hung from the main flagpole. We carried a banner and two wooden poles past the doorman. It was all wrapped in official looking blue paper so there was no challenge to this 6ft by 2ft package. We hung it over the side of the building. The paper broke up but the wood did not fall onto the street. We retired and returned later with a white sheet painted RAG, which was flown from the mast. We exited from a door on the ground floor into the electricity showroom. I remember the look of surprise on the uniformed commissionaires' faces, presumably because we had appeared from a normally unused door. We were in the street before they could react.

Although quickly removed by the building security personnel, the stunt made it into the *Evening Chronicle* with a photograph and headline suggesting that Electrical Engineering students were suspected! That was unsurprising as a telephone call had been made to the newspaper.

Late that night several statues in Newcastle were dressed up and a raid to Sunderland managed to cover billboards with 'Sunderland Rag Cancelled' signs.

John Dore and Bill Stephenson

Traffic-stopping students during 1957's Rag Procession.

Getting involved in the Rag Revue was always fun. We took over the Palace Theatre and filled it every night for a week. There were jobs for all sorts of students. Premises and sewing machines seemed to appear somehow or other and several of us beavered away to produce costumes from goodness knows what. I remember one particular act when a group of chain-swinging, tough looking guys lined up on stage to give their version of *The Teddy Bears(Boys) Picnic*. It brought the house down! One line sticks in my memory.

Each day you bet begins with Gillette and a finely sharpened edge,
Because we're nice little Teddy Boys.

It was the time when street gangs were making their presence felt, especially in southern seaside towns. Being in the audience at the Palace Theatre when Lonnie Donegan, on stage with his skiffle group, caused the audience to dance in the aisle was exciting and a bit frightening too.

Majorettes stop the traffic on Northumberland Street, 1957.

The significant things I remember about the Rag Parade were the support of the general public, the acquiescence of the University authorities and the tolerance of the police. No traffic could move in the heart of the city. During the night before the parade, a couple of bobbies were doing foot patrol down Northumberland Street when they noticed that the golden lady above the Northern Goldsmiths was being 'dressed' appropriately by a student who'd somehow managed to climb up there. No doubt some interesting comments passed between them, but then the bobbies just continued on their way! Imagine that happening now. Firms lent their flat-bed lorries and student groups worked on them to produce fantastic themed creations. The medical faculty rigged up an operating theatre with massive saws and hammers, plus, inevitably, lots of blood. I think we did something involving a dragon that wobbled its long neck over the cab of the float. The parade made its way down crowd-lined streets; success was measured in the amount of money collected into the float's buckets as they passed amongst the crowds. It was all such good natured, innocent fun and charities benefitted from it.

Elizabeth Clark (née Thompson)

Two of my treasured possessions are the 'Rag Pie' magazines of 1956 and 1957. Both have lost their covers but are otherwise intact. The 1956 one was edited by Architecture student Alan Plater, who later became rather well-known as a playwright. In one Rag we failed by, I think, about £33 to break the national record (then about £1300, which was a lot of money, about two years' starting salary for a graduate engineer) for raising money from Rag. It was very unfortunate that there were some outstanding amounts owing from advertisers at the time, which would have clinched it for us.

Tony Finn

I think this was a stunt to kidnap the President of Ethel Williams Hall (in Undergraduate gown). I don't think she minded too much!

Rag Pie, 1959.

Presumably this was the Scottish Country Dance Society. The accordion player was Bernard Dixon, a resident of Henderson Hall and in later life Editor of New Scientist. Martin Nellist

Living on a student grant

I arrived at Newcastle University Department of Education in 1955 to take an Art Teacher's Diploma. We had to attend all the lectures and tutorials that the students in the other departments had to take, and we had teaching practice two days every week. There was certainly no time for a part-time job. At the end of all this we took exactly the same papers as the students from other faculties who took the teaching qualification, but we were only awarded a 'degree equivalent' not a proper degree and were not allowed to attend the graduation ceremony.

I moved into an attic bed sitting room in a house in Framlington Place, an elegant terrace of Georgian buildings between the grounds of the RVI and the Town Moor. My room was up two flights of stairs and took up most of the top floor. The bathroom was down one flight and up another, which taught me to be careful with water, as I had to make the up and down trip with a bucket for all my drinking and cooking water. I did my washing up and washed my clothes in the bathroom when I could find it vacant, being careful to clean up the basin afterwards.

We had grants from the Local Education Authority, a good exercise in money management, as the amount was adequate if one was careful, but we never had a penny to spare.

I worked out that I could spend £4 per week, which had to cover rent, food, books, art materials, craft materials, the greedy gas meter and fares when I was on teaching practice or wanted to go home. Art and craft supplies were expensive, even second-hand text books mounted up and the rent was 25 shillings a week. I saved money by walking into town and didn't go home until half term, by bus. I did not know any students who owned cars, not many of the parents did either.

It was a cold winter and the gas pressure was low at the top of the house. I used to lie down on the floor in front of the gas fire just to keep warm, and I did my reading in bed. I had not taken to wearing trousers at that time, not many women did and tights were not yet invented; we wore very uncomfortable suspender belts and stockings. It was hard to keep warm and I added a greenhouse heater to the furniture of the room. I left it burning at night, because I couldn't afford any more shillings for the gas meter. I had to clean soot off the mesh at the top when it wasn't lit. I found that a boiled kettle gave off quite a bit of heat.

I used to buy a shilling's worth of meaty bones in the indoor market and boiled them with carrots and onions on my single-ring gas cooker. This was the basis of my main meal every day of every week. I ate it like that the first day, and added lentils, dried peas, barley, a parsnip or whatever vegetables I could get cheaply on subsequent days. I ate bread and cheese, or jam, or boiled eggs for tea.

I envied my richer friend Helen downstairs because she could actually afford sausages regularly, whereas I had them occasionally as a treat. I had not eaten breakfast for several years, not wise but cheap. We bought our bread and dried goods, even vegetables and fruit, at the little shop around the corner, as there was only time to go to the markets once a week, on a Saturday. It was only three years since rationing had ended. My weekly treat was to be invited into Helen's room to listen to *The Goon Show*.

Julie Barton

College Road with the Union on the right around 1958.

Brian Sefton

I came to King's College, from a small seaside town in north Yorkshire in 1951 and joined a very small Department of History – just 12 of us in years two and three.

My home for three years was Ethel Williams Hall; women only with strict rules about male visitors, who had to be out of rooms by 6pm. We had to obtain permission from the porter on the locked front door to come in after 11pm. On several evenings a week we had 'formal dinner' which involved wearing an academic gown. Mine was bought solely for that purpose as we didn't have to wear one to our lectures. The Hall was near Four Lane Ends from which trolley buses took us into the centre of town.

Maureen Callcott

I have a set of receipts for accommodation at Eustace Percy Hall, which was on the site that is now the Freeman Hospital. It cost £44 a term. When I first moved in there were still people living there from its previous incarnation as a Ministry of Pensions and National Insurance Hostel. Some were troubled souls who still suffered from shell shock received during the First World War.

In my second year at Eustace Percy Hall I got a rather large room. I thought it was a great improvement on my previous room, until I woke up one night with cockroaches in my hair. When I put on the light the floor was covered

Henderson Hall Ball, May 1956.

with these creatures scuttling for cover. Apparently this infestation had been going on for some time but when the previous occupant, a Polish porter, reported it no one could understand what he was talking about.

Tony Morris

Buns, bars and other distractions

I was a student at King's College, which was then still part of Durham University, from 1956 to 1959, when I graduated in chemical engineering. The main memory I have of the first year was the amazing Rag Week, which was held in the autumn term and virtually took over Newcastle City Centre. I'm pretty sure we even had Lonnie Donegan and his skiffle group performing in the Haymarket.

Various poker schools took place in the Union Common room. The same players seemed to attend every day and apparently never went to lectures. On Wednesday afternoons (which were always free of lectures and practicals) I met a group of my friends for tea and cake at Bainbridge's.

The main activity on a Saturday night was centred on the Students' Union, where there was always a dance and amazing volumes of Newcastle Brown Ale were consumed. As the vast majority of students did not own cars in those days, there were minimal restrictions on what you could drink provided you could stand up at the end.

Godfrey Arnold

Social life was centred on the 'bun room' in the Union, where a toasted teacake was lunch and a black and white TV provided the only place to watch Wimbledon, for example. Hardly anyone had TVs at home yet. The Union, SNEC (Saturday Night Entertainments Committee), was where we socialised on Saturday evenings – dancing in my case. There was a bar but most of my friends didn't drink much alcohol, though the men, especially the rugby players, certainly boasted of Saturday night binges.

Maureen Callcott

When I arrived at university, I joined all the political parties that had official societies as I wanted to broaden my political knowledge. When the officers of each party discovered this I was simultaneously thrown out of all of them. This taught me how narrow minded and humourless politicians were.

Tony Morris

The Union (right) was already too small in 1956. It had been built for about 1,200 students: in my day there were 3,300 at King's, more than all the other Durham Colleges put together.

The second floor was the refectory where you could have lunch. It was waitress service then and took forever, so my friends and I hardly ever went there: we used the 'BR' which was just down College Road from the Union and had been a British Restaurant during the war. Another eatery was The Barn, which was a prefabricated concrete building behind the Union: this

Newcastle University

257

was demolished to build the new Union extension during the 60s, after I left. In my last year, the University bought the Grand Hotel in the Haymarket and this became another place to eat.

We went every day to the Mens Bar in the Union [not in fact 'men only' but derived from 'mens agitat molem' meaning 'mind over matter'!], which was oak-panelled and had club chairs, and a wonderful atmosphere: the only woman allowed was the barmaid. I used to have a half pint of Newcastle Amber and lime and a sandwich. Those were the days when there were men's and women's common rooms on the ground floor, and men's and women's writing rooms on the first floor. The Bun Room in the basement was also the mixed bar. There were facilities to get a hot bath downstairs in the Union basement, for those whose accommodation was less well appointed.

When I had finished my Finals in 1959, and we were waiting for the results, we were asked if any of us were interested in a three-day course on the University's new computer, a Ferranti Pegasus that had been installed the previous year. Six of us took up the offer. The computer was in one of the houses in (if I remember correctly) Kensington Terrace, near the Residence of the Rector (Dr Bosanquet). It was a large pale grey box about eight feet high, eight or ten feet long and two feet deep. It took about 25kw of power to work it, and the room had to be air-conditioned to disperse the heat. We learned to program fairly simple tasks in Pegasus Autocode, then considered to be a 'high-level language'! Having written the code, it had to be punched onto paper tape, a laborious process that was fraught with errors. The machine output its results on even more paper tape, which you ran through the tape printer, hoping that what came out made sense. However, we did feel at the time that we were on the threshold of a new era, and so it proved. One of only about fifty Pegasus machines to be built to this design, it was eventually acquired by the Science Museum in London in the late 1980s.

Tony Finn

Our final exams did not mean trying to read our names on lists 'Under the Arches'. We congregated in the hall of the Medical School after the last of the *viva voce* exams. The Senior Porter would read out the names of the successful candidates in alphabetical order. If your name was not read out you crept away. Successful students then tried to find a telephone to let family and friends know before returning to pick up invitations to a sherry party later in the evening with the Dean and other members of staff. We were doctors!

Margaret Bishop (née Slater)

These splendid photos from 1955 were taken in the quadrangle where the School of Agriculture was based (in the building now occupied by Architecture). I was a young secretary in Agriculture at the time. It must have been a hard winter, the green was deep in snow and the Agric students built a huge snow cow (or was it a bull?) in front of the School. A photographer from *Newcastle Journal* took photos and it did appear in the newspaper. I remember being brought out of the office to appear on the photos.

Joan Smith (née Howe)

Joan Smith

Joan Smith

Fine Artists

Newcastle University's renowned and popular BA Fine Art was an unusual course as most art schools just offered a diploma, not a degree. The gender bias was also unusual with around half the students being women. However, discipline was strict with students expected to sign in each morning by 9.30am.

In 1956, when Brian Sefton and John Walker were students, staff included some very distinguished artists including Professor Lawrence Gowing as Director (replaced in 1959 by Professor Kenneth Rowntree). Victor Pasmore, a leading abstract artist was Master of Painting and his assistant Richard Hamilton would become 'father of Pop Art'. The Art Dept also held evening classes for the public.

Martin Nellist

Fine Art student Peter Forrester 'daubs' in the Haymarket in 1957 during Rag Week.

In 1957, a group of local artists – Ross Hickling, Bill Smith, Harry and Alan Lord – founded the Univision Gallery, located in the basement of the Royal Court Grill, Bigg Market, which was dedicated to promoting abstract art. Approaching the Univision, [fellow student] Rosemary Preece and I organised a two-person show of our abstract and semi-abstract paintings. Several of my square paintings were rotated by 45 degrees on the wall so that they became diamond-shaped.

John A. Walker (extract from 'Learning to Paint', 2003)

Top, the Univision Gallery, 1957.

Above, John Walker in his garret studio in Jesmond, 1956, with his painting 'Black Frost' in progress.

Right Brian Sefton with fellow student John Walker's 'Cubist musical instrument', around 1958.

In 1959 another Fine Art student, Peter Forrester, helped with the decor for a new coffee bar and music venue on High Bridge. The Marimba, a venture by Peter Jefferys, a former student at Newcastle University, became well-known for its classy Italian coffee, and for the jazz served up in the evenings.

Peter Forrester

An advertisement in Newcastle's *What's On* guide for June 1959 described the ambience: 'Marimba means comfort, an urbane metropolitan atmosphere, Italian cooking, Espresso coffee, American ice cream and the company you like. In High Bridge, just off Grey Street, you will find MARIMBA. The decor is based upon ancient Mexican art, you will find sculpture, mosaics, murals, pottery. After an afternoon's shopping or any time, there is no place like Marimba.'

MARIMBA *spells*

Music
Atmosphere
Relaxation
Italian Cuisine
Moderate Prices
Best Attention
Art Exhibitions

LUNCHES 12 to 3
Chef's Special 4/3

AFTERNOON
TEAS
AND
COFFEE

HIGH TEAS 4 to 6.30

30 HIGH BRIDGE STREET NEWCASTLE
(off Grey St.,)
ATMOSPHERE WITH A DIFFERENCE !!

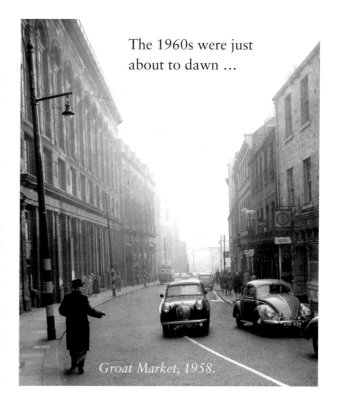

The 1960s were just about to dawn …

Groat Market, 1958.

The contributors

Looking up the Groat Market towards the Bigg Market with the old Town Hall on the right, 1956.